unWorking

EXIT THE RAT RACE,
LIVE LIKE A MILLIONAIRE,
AND BE HAPPY NOW

CLARK VANDEVENTER

Cover design by Ryan Lause

Formatted for print and eBook by Daria Lacy

Edited by Elizabeth Glass Turner

ISBN 978-0-692-45909-6

Contact the author and publisher at
unWorkingBook.com
Clark Vandeventer
Post Office Box 7172-468
Stateline, Nevada 89449

Help spread the ideas in this book
by using the hashtag #unWorkingBook
on Twitter. You can also tweet to
the author @clarkvand.

Read more of Clark's writings on lifestyle
design at FamilyTrek.org and
like Family Trek on Facebook at
facebook.com/FamilyTrek

Through many dangers, toils and snares I have already come.

'Twas grace that brought me through thus far and grace will lead me home.

To my wife,
All that I am,
All that I ever was,
Is here in your perfect eyes,
They're all I can see.

Table of Contents

Letter to My Children **5**

Jean Luc Godard said, "He who jumps into the void owes no explanation to those who stand and watch." Jean Luc Godard may have been right, but Clark's kids are not just standing by and watching. They're on the journey. The decisions Clark and his wife have made about how to live their life directly impact their children. Perhaps he does own them an explanation.

Introduction **11**

Leaving behind a succcessful career at the Reagan Ranch, Clark and his wife depart on a six month road trip with their son. Their plan was that once the journey was complete they would return home, buckle down, live respectable lives, send their kids to the right schools, serve on the right boards and live happily ever after. They set off thinking they were on sabbatical, but their sabbatical would turn into a lifestyle.

"Living epicly is like crack. Once you get a taste you can't stop; you just have to figure out a way to keep it going."

Chapter 1: From the outside looking in **19**

The life of your dreams is not about money. There are lots of people with money who are not living the life of their dreams just like there are lots of people without money who are not living the life of their dreams. It's not about the money.

Why is the life of your dreams so elusive? Can anyone live a life of their dreams, or is that kind of life only for people who are "special?" Those are theoretical questions that are "too big" for the purpose of this book. The real question is, "Do you believe a life of *your* dreams is possible?" Do you believe *you* can live a life of design?

"Most people get the highest-paying job possible and then figure out how to arrange their lives around that job. They get a job and then buy a life commensurate to their income level. To these people, one's lifestlye is determined by how much money they have. I suggest that you not arrange your life around a job, but that you arrange your life around what you value most. Get a job that fits your life, not a life that fits your job."

Chapter 2: Growing Pains **33**

Many times the path less traveled is littered with failure and humbling experiences. Learn how to use the failures in your life and embrace the freedom that comes with them. Clark talks about how defeated he felt after losing his congressional campaign and moving into his in-laws garage. He paints a picture of what life in the garage looked like and quotes JK Rowling, author of the Harry Potter series: "Rock bottom became the solid foundation from which I re-built my life."

"Losing everything was the best thing that ever happened to me. It made me realize that losing everything isn't all that bad. I was forever freed from the fear of failure. I have been freed from the things I used to

clutter my life with that I thought would make me happy. Rebuilding from nothing, I was given the opportunity to build from design."

Chapter 3: Casting a vision for your future 45

Businesses know that future success won't just happen. They need a plan. Think about your life the way you would if you were about to prepare a business plan. Stop spinning your wheels. Don't just keep trudging along. Give yourself time and space to figure out what you want. Having a vision for your future will help you do the hard work when the time for working comes, but you've got to have the vision first.

"Settling on a vision for the future is important because once you settle on a vision, you can stop wasting your time doing things that aren't helping you achieve a life of your design and focus only on those things that do."

Chapter 4: Living in the Now 65

"I wish I had retired two years sooner." Those were the words a man spoke to Clark whose wife had just been diagnosed with Alzheimer's disease. To Clark, two years seemed like a pittance. What about the rest of the years? So many people are working toward a great future, but that future is not guaranteed. The only thing we know we have for sure is today. Retirement and those promised "Golden Years" may never come; if you do reach that finish line, life may not look like you expected. Don't postpone time with your family, adventures, and living an epic life now for the hope of doing those things in the future. Learn how to live an epic life now.

"I made the decision to no longer give the best of my life to someone else and to abandon the idea of simply trading my time for money."

Chapter 5: It's hard to find a friend **79**

When you abandon the conventional life you can become very isolated; friends and even family can become distant. Many see it as a rejection of their life, some are jealous, some just don't understand. Learn how to seek out people who support your new life, deal with those who don't and let go of the ones who will never understand.

"I felt terribly alone living in my in-laws' garage. My relationship with my wife and kids was strong, but everyone else was gone. Although Monica and I were full of hope regarding our future, I also struggled with waves of depression. I'd sit in the garage at night reading and drinking cheap whiskey, wondering what happened to everyone. I felt like I had lots of friends when I was a big shot... Where were all those people now?"

Chapter 6: It ain't always easy **97**

It ain't always easy! Don't jump off into the abyss and think that everything is going to work out perfectly. Great stories don't develop that way, and you want your story to be great! We all have to prepare for the hard times. Here is an honest picture of some hard times Clark and his family faced. Before you throw caution to the wind, count the costs.

"I feel very strongly that I need to communicate how precarious our situation is at times because I don't want to paint too rosy a picture, have you throw caution to the wind... and then blame me for not telling you how hard this is! It's hard, but it's totally worth it"

Chapter 7: Let's Make a Deal **107**

Whatever we have in life, we have because we have traded a part of our life to get it. We trade a part of our life to get money, and then we trade our money to get stuff. To put it directly, whatever we have in life, we have because we trade a part of our life to get it. How much of your life are you willing to trade to get what you want? There's no right or wrong answer to this question. The only wrong answer is to not address the question at all. You want to make sure you spend your life energy wisely.

"Time is of infinite value. If I'm going to trade a part of my life for something, I'd better make darn sure that I want it. I want to make a good trade."

Chapter 8: Patchwork Income **119**

Living a different life requires different thinking about how you make money. Clark and his wife have developed a system that provides flexibility and freedom which they call "Patchwork Income." Patchwork Income is different from "freelance" or being a "consultant" and provides much greater financial security than "getting a job." Patchwork Income brings the idea of diversification to income. If diversification is such a good idea for retirement savings, why not bring the idea to income?

"Once we realized what we were doing -- how we had accidentally started building this amazing patchwork -- I determined that I would never depend on a single source of income for our family. We would make a beautiful patchwork."

Chapter 9: Choose Your Risk **129**

Nothing in life is guaranteed. If you have a good job there is no guarantee you will have it tomorrow. The old economic system was built on the idea that if you were loyal to your employer they would be loyal to you. This idea is dead. Move on. Experiment with new things and find work you love. Don't fall into the trap of thinking you are being selfish by pursuing work you love. Pursuing work that you love will make you come alive. Just as important, there's a gift in you that you have the opportunity to give to the world. Don't hold back. Give it.

"It may sound scary to 'go for it', but it's no more risky than staying in a job you don't love. There is no security in the job market today. There's no such thing anymore as a safe or secure job. Your choice is not between playing it safe and taking a risk. Your choice is between risk that is unsatisfying or risk that satisfies."

Chapter 10: Eat, Talk, Make Love. 139

If you are married or in a committed relationship, accomplishng your goals in life will be almost impossible if you and your partner are not of one heart and one mind. Learn how to be of one heart and one mind with your partner despite wild changes in your life. Challenge tradtional gender roles and rethink income generation and household responsibilities. Studies show that couples where both partners share these responsibilities have more sex than couples where there's a division of these areas.

"I'm not sure which comes first - sharing household responsibilities creating good vibes or sharing household responsibilities growing out of a shared life. Whichever it is, who's going to argue with more sex?"

Chapter 11: Family > Career. 153

You've heard the expression, "Nobody ever said on their death-bed that they wish they'd worked more." People say this and shrug their shoulders like there's nothing they can do about it. There is something they can do about it! Live a life where work and family are intertwined. Most people are *working and* **unLiving.** Start *living and* **un**Working.

"Slowly the chase for a new career or business opportunity or more money began to take a back seat to lifestyle."

Chapter 12: unSchooling and unWorking **167**

Our world has changed, but the way we view both work and school has not changed. School today looks the same as it has for decades and the model is outdated. The future of work is unWorking and education today should be designed to meet the needs of tomorrow. By unWorking, we remove ourselves from the rat race. By unSchooling or hack-schooling, we get our kids out of the minaturied, pressurized rat race.

"For me, the line between what is recreation and what is work can often be very blurry. What's fun and what's work isn't defined by punching a time clock. Why should it be any different for my kids? Why should I think that in order for them to learn, they have to be at a school? If I don't go to an office to work, why should they go to a school to learn?"

Chapter 13: Go a little crazy **181**

Society has labeled certain aspirations as ridiculous because there's not much potential to make a lot of money. These aspirations aren't ridiculous if your goal is happiness and fulfillment. Rethink your definition of success. Learn about "the hypomanic edge" and how people who are "just a little crazy" tend to be successful.

"When we're kids, dreaming comes naturally. Our imaginations run wild and everything is possible. Over time, our schools and our consumerist culture beat the dreamer into submission. We're taught to think according to career counselors. We begin thinking less about what we love or what we were born to do and more about meeting market demands or how much money we can make at a profession. We need to learn to dream again"

Chapter 14: Live Epicly Now **193**

Make the most of what you have now. Don't wait to be happy until you have things right. You will not be happy in the future if you can't figure out how to be happy now.   Small steps in your current life can bring new perspective. If you live in the mountains, enjoy the mountains. If you live at the beach, enjoy the beach. If you live in an incredible cultural center, enjoy the culture.   Be interesting. This really goes beyond where we live and the recreation we choose. This is about our entire life energy and where we spend it and how we spend it.

"Make the most of your life, wherever you are, right now. Whatever you may want life to look like in the future, you can be that person today with every choice you make."

Exhortation **203**

ex·hor·ta·tion, ˌegzôrˈtāSHən, ˌeksôr-/ *noun*

1. an address or communication emphatically urging someone to do something.

Epicly or Epically. **207**

Who Needs to Read unWorking? **209**

Acknowledgements **215**

From the Blog **219**

Hi, I'm Clark. I'm from the future, and it's amazing.

We live in a post Great Recession world where there's no such thing as a secure job anymore. Don't complain. Just adapt.

For a long time our society has been set-up for a certain way of living. That's why there are so many W-2 employees in the United States. Our culture has needed people to go to work, go into debt and send their kids to school.

That's not the future.

The future is one of flexibility and customization. Freelance is a word we'll hear more and more. My wife Monica and I are early adapters of the emerging world; we are ahead of the curve. Life will get easier for us not just because we'll get better at this life, but because the emerging world will accommodate our lifestyle. We're weird now, but we're the future normal.

unWorking is a guidebook for anyone who's taken a few hard knocks in life. Perhaps you sense the rules have changed, but you can't really make sense of it all. You've been looking for someone who can explain what's happened and this book does that.

This book also deals with the nitty-gritty details of life, like how to make money in the emerging world through patchwork income, questions about school for your kids and the future of education, marriage, gender roles and balancing work and family. I also sort through the hurt and loneliness I experienced, and maybe you have as well, if you also have found yourself unemployed or under-employed.

1

This book is must-reading for anyone who's ever wanted to quit their job but keeps letting the years pass by due to fear. According to the Bureau of Labor Statistics, in 2013 an average of 53,436 people were laid off every single day. That's a lot of people being laid off every day, but it was actually fewer than any year since 2001. When someone has just lost their job, they are forced to do something they wouldn't have otherwise done: evaluate their life. They can either do a cursory evaluation or they can dig deep. unWorking is for the people who want to dig deep.

For those within the workforce the situation is even more depressing. In a massive report released by Gallup in 2013, it was stated that only 13 percent of workers feel engaged with their jobs, meaning they feel a sense of passion for their work, a deep connection to their employer and spend their days driving innovation and moving their company forward. The vast majority however, some 63 percent, are "not engaged," meaning they are unhappy but not drastically so. In short, they have checked out. They sleepwalk through their days putting little energy into their work. A full 24 percent are what Gallup calls "actively disengaged," meaning they pretty much hate their jobs. They act out and undermine what their coworkers accomplish.

Add the last two categories and you get 87 percent of workers worldwide who, as Gallup puts it, "are emotionally disconnected from their workplaces and less likely to be productive." In other words, work is more often a source of frustration than one of fulfillment for nearly 9 out of 10 of the world's workers.

Life was meant to be more than listening to eight different bosses drone on about mission statements. That's why the future is about unWorking.

You were made for so much more.

Achieving the sort of lifestyle design that my wife and I have achieved for our family has not been easy. If I wanted easy, I'd go get a job. I may be like 87 percent of the world's workforce and be mentally checked out, but it'd be easy.

This book isn't about easy. Few things worth achieving are easy.

I want to help you live epicly.

Let's go on a journey together.

Clark Vandeventer
Lake Tahoe, March 21, 2015

Letter to my children:

To my children,

Jean Luc Godard may have been right when he said that he who jumps into the void owes no explanation to those who stand and watch. I'd like to offer some explanation to you, though, because you are not just standing by and watching. You travel the journey with us. The decisions your mom and I have made about our life directly impact you.

I think I do owe you an explanation.

Life is an epic journey. I've always lived with that sense and I hope you will come to as well. I think that is one thing that keeps you going when you face dark chapters. When you live with a sense of purpose it puts trials in perspective. I've never read a great novel or a biography of a remarkable person whose life was a continuous upward trajectory.

Perhaps this is a dark and gloomy place to start. Maybe it'd be nicer if I started off by talking about the good times. But it's best that you know right from the start that life is not always easy. There is pain and heartache and disappointment. There will come a day when your dreams will be shattered. One day the world will look at you as a success and the next day you'll be viewed as a failure. People are fickle. You will find that someone you thought was your friend is not. Someone you love will die.

I have known both success and failure. Neither triumph nor disaster have been stranger to me. Had I written this letter to you when I was a bit younger and when I'd only ever really known success, I could have never begun by talking about hard times or heartache because I knew so little about those things.

Some of the hard times your mom and I have faced have changed the way we look at other people. I've become a more compassionate and forgiving person. I've become more patient with myself and with others. I think these humbling experiences made me a better dad.

The things I believed about life during my 20's were the same things a lot of people believed about our world: Things are better today than they've ever been. Tomorrow will be better. The economy was humming along. Money was easy to come by and easy to spend. For me, from the time I was in high school and then into college and then beginning my career -- every year was better than the year before. Every year I enjoyed more success. Every year I had more freedom. Every year I made more money.

Shortly after your mom and I were married I remember going on a walk with her and talking about where we each were in our careers. I told her that we'd never have to worry about money again. It didn't matter that we were living paycheck to paycheck because I thought we would always have a paycheck.

I grew up in the 1980s, a time of almost unparalleled economic growth and prosperity. There was a brief period of recession in the early 1990s and my parents lost their house. I remember my parents being upset about losing their house, but for me I don't remember that being a hard time. My lasting impression of that experience was that it was a time of adventure because we moved out of the main part of town and into the country.

My generation had no clue what was about to hit us as the early birth pangs of the Great Recession began to emerge in early 2008, which also happens to be the time that I made a decision that would change my life forever.

Many of the difficult realities I've faced in life have come about as a result of my own choices. I could have remained on my comfortable, familiar track. Likely I would have continued to advance in my career. It's almost certain I would have continued to make more money.

But I became convinced if I stayed on that path, all that'd eventually be left of me would be a shell of a man. I'm not saying everyone who is on the corporate track with a 401(k) is a sell-out. But it was not for me. It was not what I was made to do. It was not what I wanted to give my life to. For me to keep going just because of a paycheck and a measure of perceived security -- I saw no way to continue on that path without waking up every morning and feeling empty inside. I didn't want to brush aside my dreams, give the best years of my life to a job and then wake up at 65 and wonder what the hell happened to my life.

I was 27 years old. I had an enviable job. I quit.

In some ways it was an easy decision. I felt like I had to do it. I really, really had to do it. In another way, it was the most difficult decision of my life. It was a decision that has had huge ramifications. That decision, along with the continuing decision to embrace it, has shaped our family life as much or more than any other.

Your mom has been my great support on this journey. She has been my partner and I have been hers. Our life after I turned in that letter of resignation became a whirlwind. After years of only knowing success and triumph and exultation, that decision ushered in a season of failure, disaster and despair. That's what people saw from the outside looking in, at least. I felt that way on the inside a lot of times, too. We had fun during that season of our life though, because we view life as a great adventure. We descended into the abyss with hope. Still, there were moments of doubt, even severe doubt, that were some of the darkest of our life.

The night before I was going to quit my job I started having doubts. Your mom said to me: *"If it's the money, quit. If there are other reasons you're thinking about not doing this, okay -- maybe wait and sort through that stuff. But if it's just the money, quit. We'll figure it out."*

I know men who have said things to me like:

"If I were single I'd go for it. I'd quit my job and...."

"I'd like to start my own business, but with the wife and kids I can't afford to take the risk."

"I really want to... but my wife thinks it's too much of a risk."

I think the exact opposite may be true for me. I don't know if I would have ever summoned the courage to forge my own trail had it not been for your mom. I think there's a good chance I'd still be in the same job doing the same thing.

Sadly, I have observed very few of what I would call really exciting marriages. Your mom and I believe we have one. We're in love, and not just in a hazy-eyed sense. We are looking together in the same direction. Life is already too hard to spend any time fighting with the person who is supposed to be your partner.

In time, we would lose just about everything. We lost our house and our status and our egos. The only thing that would have been worse? Betraying myself. Selling out. Becoming a shell of a man.

That's what I want you to know.

I want you to follow your dreams, as crazy as those dreams may seem. The worst that can happen is that you'll lose everything. If you do, you'll realize losing everything isn't that bad.

So kids, this is not a self-help book. This is not a book about success or failure or about work or figuring out your career. This book is not about money or the things that money can buy.

This book is about helping you, and anyone who reads it, figure out what you want your life to look like. This book is an attempt to help you figure out what you value most and then discover how you can arrange life to accurately reflect those values. This book is about understanding and thriving in the ~~emerging~~ already here world.

I believe we each have something special to offer this world and that there's a particular way each of us are wired to live. Instead of figuring out what we have to offer or what our wiring looks like, most of us think about money and getting a job that can pay us the most money.

My hope for you isn't that you make a ton of money. I want you to have a great life. Living life the way you're wired to live it will bring you more happiness and joy than all the riches of Babylon.

As I sit down to write these words to you, my children, you are each very small. Because you are so young, your mom and I must give you almost constant instruction. Everything you know today you know because we have either taught you those things or you have observed them from us or others we have exposed you to. In word and deed, we are your instructors.

My heart's desire is that by the time you're old enough to read these words, I will have been able to transition from the role of instructor and into the role of advisor. I choose that word carefully. I did not choose the word coach because on a team it is the coach, not the players, who is ultimately in charge.

But CEOs of major corporations have advisers. Even the President of the United States has advisers. The president listens, takes it all in, and processes it. It's the president, not the advisers, who makes the decision. You have to be the president of your life.

I write boldly. Occasionally, I may come on strong. My aggressiveness is driven by a determination to live an examined life. I want to be thoughtful about the way I live. I want to be thoughtful about the lessons I instill in you.

I've jumped into the void. This book explains why.

Love,

Dad

Introduction:

I handed in my resignation letter the first week of 2008, just as the early birth pangs of the Great Recession were being felt. A year later, not much had gone as planned. I had quit my job to buy a cafe in Santa Barbara, California, where we were living, but after months of negotiations, the cafe was sold to a different buyer.

I didn't have a backup plan in the event the cafe didn't work out. I scrambled and began trying to build a consulting business. In six months, we were out of money and for a few months my in-laws kept us afloat. Within about eight months, though, things were coming together and I was making pretty good money as a consultant.

Because I didn't need to go to an office everyday -- I worked with a phone and a laptop and hopped on a plane a few times a month -- my wife and I decided to take advantage of our freedom. I was on a chairlift in Lake Tahoe at Heavenly Mountain the week of

Christmas 2008 when the idea occurred to me. We would rent out our house and travel. When I get an idea that really captivates me, I move fast. Just after Christmas I began advertising that our house was available for lease. Within a few days we had a signed lease from ideal renters. In February of 2009, just a little more than a year after I had quit my job, we packed up our car and our 15-month-old son Jackson to depart on a six month road trip.

Driving north from Santa Barbara, we planned to spend three weeks in Lake Tahoe before journeying eastward across the United States to Washington, D.C. Once we reached the East Coast, we'd move westward again and eventually return to Santa Barbara.

I believe a warning is in order:

If you are considering a "sabbatical" from life as you've lived it, know that sometimes sabbaticals have a way of turning into a life-style. Living epicly is like crack. Once you get a taste you can't stop; you just have to figure out a way to keep it going.

When we departed on that road trip we viewed the next six months as an interlude in our life. I would continue working but work was less important than the adventure. Once our journey was complete we would return to Santa Barbara and buckle down, live respectable lives, send our kids to the right schools, serve on the right boards and live happily ever after.

At the end of six months on the road we returned home to Santa Barbara. Another six months later, I announced I was a candidate for United States Congress.

I lost.

Two months later, with my wife and now two kids, I moved into my in-laws garage. Talk about a whirlwind.

It was a very embarrassing time for me personally and I retreated from many relationships. All the people who told me I was crazy when I'd quit my job were being proven right.

I was twenty-one years old when I graduated from college and moved to California where I took a job I'd been groomed for at the Reagan Ranch, the home of the 40th President of the United States, Ronald Reagan. The ranch was being preserved in the tradition of other presidential homes like George Washington's Mount Vernon or Thomas Jefferson's Monticello. Over the years I worked with men and women who'd served at the highest levels of government. I exchanged Christmas cards with people like former United States Attorney General Ed Meese.

By the time I was twenty-six years old, I was the deputy director the Reagan Ranch. I had raised millions and millions of dollars from philanthropists to preserve the former president's home and build the Reagan Ranch Center in Santa Barbara. Saying things like, "I'd like you to consider a gift of one million dollars," while sipping a Grey Goose martini was not uncommon for me. I visited donors on their yachts, flew on their planes and often found myself staying at some of the most luxurious hotels in the United States.

Jerold Panas, one of the most renowned fundraisers of our time, referred to me as a star. I could pick up the phone and call a United States Senator or a Fortune 500 CEO and they'd take my call. I worked with a lot of rich, famous and powerful people. The first time I heard the name Sarah Palin was when she had just taken office as Governor of Alaska in 2006. At that time I was told she would likely be the next Republican Vice Presidential candidate, more than two years before the rest of world was introduced to her.

When I ran for Congress, I was asked in an interview what member of Congress past or present I most admired. I answered Jack Kemp, the former Buffalo Bills Quarterback turned politician. After serving in Congress, Jack Kemp went on to serve as Secretary of Health and Human Services in the Administration of the first President Bush and would later be a Republican Vice Presidential candidate. When I gave the answer Jack Kemp, it wasn't just because of what I'd read about the guy; it was personal experience from the time we spent together.

My wife and I had a great life. When I say that I had an "enviable" job or that I made "good" money, I don't want you to just think I had a good corporate job with anonymity. I was kind of a "big deal." Though I had given up my job at the Reagan Ranch, as a consultant I ran in the same circles. As a congressional candidate I did as well. Then in what seems like the blink of an eye I was living in my in-laws garage.

I had bet it all on winning my election. I cashed out my retirement for living expenses so I could be a full-time candidate, and then as a full-time candidate completely stopped my consulting work. If anyone is looking for a manual on how to go from rising political star to living in your in-laws garage, I can write it.

When we moved into my in-laws garage we had little idea what we wanted in life. We knew we didn't want to live in the garage forever, but still, we didn't really know what we wanted long-term.

When we moved into the garage, my in-laws gave me more than a roof over my family's head. They gave me time.

Let me tell you what I did with that time.

I slept in.

I think it's important I establish some trust with you up front. While it may sound good to say that after my first night of sleep in the garage I got up at 5:00 in the morning and began working on a plan, it would not be true. For the first few weeks I slept. I think I was still recovering from the emotion of my election and trying to let it sink in that I actually was living in my in-laws garage.

My daughter, who was not yet one year old when we moved in, slept in a crib just a few feet away from me. She'd wake up in the morning and wait for me to stir. Each morning, when I finally sat up and put my feet on the floor, she would clap. I remember thinking at the time, "I have no money and I live in my in-laws garage, but my daughter still claps for me when I get out of bed in the morning."

My son was now three years old, and other than the first two months of his life, as long as he had been alive, I had been around. I had been working but I did not get up and go to a job all day, five or six days a week. I was thankful for the extent to which I was able to be present the first three years of his life. Living in that garage, I began to think about how I could continue to be present every day in my kids' lives. I thought about going back to the grind and thought about what I would miss. Not only would I not be present for my daughter the way I had been for my son, but I would not be present for either of them moving forward.

I wanted to be both a full-time bread winner and a full-time dad. I didn't know how to do it yet, but I was starting to sense that getting a job wasn't the answer.

After five months in the garage we moved to Tahoe during the winter of 2010-11. My wife's grandfather had a cabin we could stay in while we continued to figure out life and build our income again, which we were clumsily doing. More importantly, we were learning.

That winter was such a special time for our family. We had our own space again, even if it was borrowed, and we enjoyed family meals with just the four of us. At night, after the kids went to bed, Monica and I would talk about our dreams. We talked about what it would take for us to be able to have two homes -- one in Santa Barbara and one in Tahoe. Remember, at that time we were still broke. We were living off the charity of others. A home in Santa Barbara and a home in Tahoe did not feel out of reach, though. We just had to decide what we really wanted, and then go for it.

We had no idea at the time what a life-altering exercise we were going through. We re-thought everything and came up with new answers to everything. We were on the verge of re-inventing our lives.

This book is about that process.

We didn't know it then, but those conversations were about exiting the rat race, living like millionaires, and being happy, now. We also sensed that we couldn't just go off the old playbook. We couldn't do what our parents generation had done because the world had changed.

In this book you'll find talk about loneliness, depression and failure. This book is about how hard times affect relationships. It's about marriage, kids, vacuuming and sex. It's about losing everything and then figuring out how to rebuild your life on the foundation of the things you value most.

I also happen to think it's a darn good story, one of epic proportions, just like yours can be.

"A man with a half volition goes back and forth and makes no progress on even the smoothest road, whereas a person with a full volition moves ahead steadily no matter how difficult the path."

Thomas Carlyle

CHAPTER 1

From the Outside Looking In

It was a cold morning -- bitterly cold -- but not the kind of cold from which I cower. This was the kind of cold that I embrace. Snow blanketed the mountain, creating a winter wonderland playground. For me, it was just another day on the slopes, just another "everyday amazing" day.

I sat down on the chairlift to head to the top of the mountain and began chatting with the person next to me. As is often the case, when my chairlift companion found out that I call Lake Tahoe home, he oozed with envy.

"I wish I could figure out a way to live here," he said wistfully.

When he learned that I ski about 60 days or more each season and spend nearly as many at the beach in the summer, he was really intrigued. He asked what I did to make money, and I began explaining to him my patchwork of income.

Then he said, *"I wish I could figure out a way to live how you live."*

Now I had a challenge. I could tell I was speaking to a professional -- a businessman -- and that he was smart. Looking at the guy I thought "that could have been me" a few years, a couple of unsuccessful business ventures and one unsuccessful congressional campaign before I moved to Tahoe and reinvented my life. The guy riding on the chairlift next to me had just expressed an interest in doing exactly what I did. I wanted to help.

I began trying to figure out what he did for a living. What was his career background, I queried? What were his professional areas of expertise? What did he know how to do and how could he adjust some things to make life in the mountains possible for him, too?

As I previously shared, I've worked with a lot of successful people in business, politics and culture. People who have been really successful will often understate their credentials. They know who they are and they're comfortable in their own skin, which is the opposite of the insecure underling who states his professional responsibilities in grandiose terms. That's why the first draft of my book didn't include much detail about my career at the Reagan Ranch. My editor pulled those details out of me and got me to do all that name dropping.

This guy was really low-key when I asked him about his career. Because my professional background also makes me an expert in asking questions and probing beneath the surface, he wasn't going to get off that easy. I asked another question and then another.

When you're on a chairlift, you don't have all that much time, but fortunately, my chairlift companion and I both unloaded and skied right up to another chairlift to go to the top of the mountain. I would have a few more minutes with the man who wanted a life like mine. I offered a bit more of my background, which made my chairlift companion feel a little more comfortable with me and then I asked the question that led him to unveil his true identity.

The ski slopes are an interesting place because of the mixture of people's backgrounds and socioeconomic status. From broke college students to rock stars, it's hard to tell the difference when everyone is bundled up, faces hidden behind goggles.

I talked for another minute with my chairlift companion about how I had pulled off my Tahoe life. I encouraged him to keep coming back and asked him to look me up when he did. As we neared the top and prepared to unload, we finally exchanged names and I told him how to find my blog.

I knew I wouldn't have any trouble finding him. He was one of the first dozen employees and a senior executive at Netflix.

◆

CAN ANYONE LIVE A LIFE OF THEIR OWN DESIGN?

That conversation we shared has been re-played over and over and over again in my head. There I was talking with someone who's made millions of dollars who was saying to me, *"How do you do it because I want to live like you."* He had a million dollars but I was the one living like a millionaire.

That guy could do it tomorrow. Cash out, walk away, move to the mountains. Start skiing. That's how easy it could be. No conversation I've ever had has more powerfully made me realize how elusive "the life of your dreams" is to most people.

If that guy feels powerless to create a life of his own design, what about the guy with a wife and two kids who's trudging along in a dead-end job making $29,000 a year?

Is living the life of your dreams a realistic goal for everyone?

Or am I special?

A good friend of mine whom I'll call Bryan (because that's his name and that's what everyone calls him) would say that I'm special. Bryan is a successful, self-employed entrepreneur and I think he would say that he's special, too.

I'm not going to tell you that everyone can live the life of their dreams. This is not just another book that's here to make everyone feel all warm and fuzzy inside.

Can anyone live the life of his or her dreams?

I don't know.

That's my answer. I really don't know.

But I believe that I can live the life of my dreams. I believe a life of my own design is possible.

What about you?

I'm not asking you what you think of anyone else. This isn't a theoretical discussion about life in general. Forget the, *"Wouldn't society break down if everyone did this?"* arguments. This is a question about you.

What about you?

Do you believe that you can live the life of your dreams? Do you believe you can live a life of your own design?

Maybe you don't. Maybe life just hasn't worked out for you and you feel like a victim of your circumstances. If you believe that, I hope you'll continue reading because while I don't know if it is possible for everyone to live the life of their dreams, I certainly believe it's possible for far more people than just me.

The time my in-laws gave me by allowing us to live in their garage and then the time we had in the Tahoe cabin that winter gave us the ability to really step back and re-think our life. In many countries, the idea of a "Gap Year" is quite common. People take a year off from work to get the space they need to evaluate their life. In the United States, we really have no such tradition. We're taught to put our head down and get to work. If we find ourselves out of work, we're supposed to pound the pavement and find another job as soon as possible. There's no time to gain perspective. There's no time to evaluate life the way Monica and I did.

The recent economic upheaval we've experienced in our society has forced many more people to ask the kind of questions Monica and I did while sitting in the garage or by the fire in Tahoe.

I get excited when a friend tells me they've lost their job. Maybe you think that sounds terrible, but it's hard to force yourself to evaluate your life when an employer is depositing thousands of dollars into your back account on a regular basis and paying for your family's healthcare. They call it the golden handcuffs. You actually have the key but won't unlock them yourself because they're so pretty. If the handcuffs are taken from you, all the sudden you can use your hands again. Will you wave your arms in the air or will you look for someone else who will give you another pair of golden handcuffs?

◆

GETTING YOUR MONEY'S WORTH

You just got laid off, you don't know how you're going to pay your bills, and I'm the jerk telling you that this is great! Maybe after being beaten up by life, just the sound of those words, "the life of your dreams," is a little intimidating. Maybe from where you're sitting today it's terrifying to even think about such a lofty goal.

So, what do you want?

Maybe that's a less intimidating way to look at it.

What do you want your life to look like? What kind of house would you like to have? Do you want a house? What kind of car do you want to drive? Do you want a car?

Those questions are surface level questions. Think about them, but I'd rather you ask yourself questions like:

- *What do I want my days to look like?*
- *What makes me happy?*
- *What am I wired to do?*

How hard are you wiling to work to get whatever it is you say you want? Whatever we have in life we get by trading our time, therefore everything we possess we have gained by trading a part of our lives to get it.

Just how much of your life are you willing to trade for a house, a car, clothes, recreation, travel? There are no right or wrong answers to these questions. I'm asking you, "How much do you value these things?"

I have a goal to ski 60+ days each winter. I also have a goal to be a present husband and father. Additionally, I want to be free to travel for weeks or months at a time. Therefore, it does not matter how much money you are willing to pay me, if you offer me a job that requires me to be present five days a week or more and 40 hours a week or more, taking that job would be counterproductive to me achieving my goals.

I want to really drive this point home because most people do not think about life in these terms. *Most people get the highest-paying job possible and then figure out how to arrange their lives around that job.* They get a job and then buy a life commensurate to their income level. To these people, one's lifestlye is determined by how much money they have.

I suggest that you not arrange your life around a job, but that you arrange your life around what you value most. Get a job that fits your life, not a life that fits your job.

It would be physically impossible for me to be present with my family to the extent I want to be present, to ski 60+ days a year, and to physically go to a job five days a week or more. It's physically impossible; it can't be done.

So how much do you want to pay me? $50,000 a year? $100,000 a year? $250,000 a year? $500,000 a year? $1 Million a year? It does not matter how much money it is; the job does not help me achieve my goals. My goal is not to make as much money as possible in order to have the best life that money can buy. My goal is to design a great life, and then figure out how to make the amount of money I need to live that life.

◆

WHAT A GUY WANTS

When you begin to think about life this way the whole world opens up to you. A life of your own design -- the life of your dreams -- begins to feel possible.

But what about the Netflix guy?

Based only on the few minutes we spent together riding a chairlift to the top of a mountain, I'm not willing to say he's not living the life of his dreams.

My wife and I have friends in Santa Barbara who own a beautiful home in Montecito, which is one of the most expensive and exclusive communities in the world. It's where Oprah lives. Our friends don't just have a home; they have acres and acres of fruit trees, gardens, aviaries and botanical gardens. They have an enormous wine cellar and every corner of the home is beautifully furnished. Their home is absolutely amazing.

I used to go to their house and think, *"I like this. I could live here. I wish...."*

I was like the Netflix guy. *"I wish I could figure out a way to have a house like this."*

The thing is, I never *really* wanted it. Sure, it'd be nice, but I know I'm not willing to do what it *really* takes to get it just like that Netflix guy isn't *really* willing to do what it takes to have my life.

The reason I'm not willing to go after that house in Montecito is because that house does not ultimately line up with what I value most. The reason that Netflix guy doesn't have my life is because ultimately, he doesn't want my life.

I'm thankful everyone doesn't want my life. As a Netflix customer, I'm thankful some people have devoted their careers to building a company that can deliver such a great service. I can admire the work of the men and women who've built Netflix and I can marvel at my friends' house in Montecito. Those aren't my dreams though.

What I suspect that guy from Netflix was trying to say is, "Wow, the way you're living your life is so cool." If he really wants to live like me though, he ought to do it, because he can.

You don't need the ability to cash out in order to re-invent your life, though. When my wife and I began building this life, there was no cashing out. We were broke.

Figuring out what you want is the first step.

What do you and your partner want your life together to look like?

For my wife and me, our time in the garage and in grandpa's cabin in Tahoe were the beginning stages of reinventing our life. At the time, we were making virtually no money. I want to use actual numbers here because the phrase, "I don't have much money," is a relative term. In the month of December 2010, a month before we headed north to Lake Tahoe for the winter in grandpa's cabin, we made $217. Where we used to have wealth, we now had no savings, no assets and a big pile of debt.

All we had was a very faint knowledge of what we wanted, the desire to achieve a certain kind of life, and enough smarts to say no to anything that ultimately would not help us achieve that life. But that was enough.

Can anyone do it?

I don't know.

We did it with $217.

I suspect the kind of person who would pick up this book can live a life of his or her own design. I have a hunch that you have what it takes to live the life of your dreams.

The Big Take-Aways

My friends' house in Montecito is what the "life of your dreams" is "supposed" to look like. Maybe you've fallen into the trap of thinking that's how you should measure success. Is the big house with a fancy car your dream though? It's okay if it is. I'm not judging the rightness or wrongness of what you value in life. The question is, "What do you value?"

In thinking about how to design your life, if you're thinking only about what your house would look like or what kind of car you'd like to drive, you're thinking way too small. Think bigger! What do you want to do with your time. What do you want to give your life to? What do you want a typical day/week/month/year in your life to look like? Again, there's no right or wrong answer. I believe Steve Jobs found an immense amount of joy and satisfaction in building Apple. I believe he was doing what he was wired to do. I find joy and satisfaction in my work and lifestlye design. I believe I am doing what I am wired to do. The amount of money Steve Jobs made is a whole lot more than the amount of money I make, but money isn't the ultimate measure of success. On the happiness scale, we are equals.

The life of your dreams is not about money. There are lots of people with money who are not living the life of their dreams just like there are lots of people without money who are not living the life of their dreams. It's not about the money.

You certainly don't need to start with a lot of money to pursue the life of your dreams. Money can actually complicate things. If you start with nothing, it's easy to build by design.

Action Steps

1. Ask yourself what you want to do when you retire. Why couldn't you do it now? Forget money, career paths and societal expectations. Think outside the box about how you could actually do now the things you've always thought about doing when you retire.

2. Make a list of the 5 things you value most. Now look at your budget. Where is your money going? Are you spending your money on the things you say you value most? Remember, you got all that money by trading part of your life to get it. If the top line items in your budget don't line up with the things you say you value most, that means you are giving your life to things that don't really matter to you.

3. Take out a pen and paper and write down your "best days" from the past year. What did you do on those days you felt most

alive? Ask yourself how you can arrange your life to have more days like those.

4. Talk with your spouse. Are you on the same page? Do you want the same things? Remember, you married a person, not a paycheck or their status.

"Though He slay me, yet will I trust Him."

Job

CHAPTER 2

Growing Pains

It's hard for me to tell you how defeated I felt when we left the garage and headed to Tahoe at the beginning of 2011. I arrived in Tahoe a broken man. I wasn't just broke in the sense that we had no money; I was broken.

In the early years of my career it seemed that everything I touched turned to gold. Life worked for me. I won't say that everything came easily because I worked hard, but it felt easy.

And then I faced a string of failures that culminated with me moving my wife and two kids into my in-laws garage. In less than two months, I went from being an up-and-coming political force and candidate for United States Congress to loading up cardboard boxes and moving in with my in-laws.

I felt terribly alone in that garage. My world shrank. We went from our beautiful condo in Santa Barbara with a community pool, tennis courts, gardens, and clubhouse to a 400 square foot garage where we'd hung canvass on the ceiling to hide the rafters and laid rugs on the concrete floor. We attempted to seal the garage door and vents to keep out the rodents who'd used the garage as a residence over the years. The garage was detached from the house and had no bathroom. There was one little window and a few florescent lights that worked sort of haphazardly. We framed walls and hung drywall to create a little room for our son Jackson and built a closet adjacent to our bed that was large enough to fit a crib for our daughter Emery, who was still less than a year old at the time.

My phone stopped ringing and I felt like my friends had forgotten me. When we moved into the garage we had a large bucket of change that we'd dip into occasionally to go out for a cup of coffee. Slowly that bucket of change disappeared. Monica started finding gigs on-line that would pay $5 for about an hour of work. The elegant dinner parties we used to host at our home were a distant memory. Trips to the Farmers Market and the art of cooking, something that we'd once viewed as a way of life, were replaced by sitting at the family dinner table and being thankful for whatever was being served. My in-laws, who had graciously taken us in, were also struggling financially at the time. There were lots of dinners consisting of ramen noodles and hot dogs.

Though we were blessed by the generosity of Monica's parents, I felt alone in a house full of people. At night I'd sit in the garage reading and drinking cheap whiskey. Lying in bed before we fell asleep I'd say to my wife, "It's just you and me."

I had no regrets about the decision to quit my job at the Reagan Ranch, the career choices I had made, or my decision to run for Congress. Each step along the way, I felt I was following my heart and God's leading in my life as best I could. I saw no way that I could have followed God's leading in my life and not be in that garage. The prayer of Job became my own, "Though He slay me, still will I trust Him."

I felt slain.

I was desperate and ready to grasp at anything. Then, in one single day, I got three phone calls. Three different people wanted to talk to me because they needed someone and they thought I was the guy.

My mind went to work on the life we could create with each of these opportunities.

I had been feeling so down and the thought that I may get one of these jobs made me feel alive again. Although I had a preference for one of the jobs, all three of them were uniquely exciting.

I was ready to pull the trigger.

My wife hesitated.

In the action steps at the conclusion of chapter one, I ask whether you and your partner are on the same page. Monica and I are on the same page. She married me, not my status or my paycheck. If she was interested in my status or my paycheck, she would have said, "Get on a plane. Get one of those jobs. We can have our life back."

That's not what she said.

Monica hesitated because she saw how each of these opportunities would take away from the parts of our life we had come to enjoy over the past few years, even during our time in the garage. It had now been three years since I quit my job at the Reagan Ranch. Even though I'd been working as a consultant, I didn't go to an office everyday. I was able to be a present husband and father. Did I really want to go back to the grind? Wasn't there a way we could figure out how to maintain the freedom and flexibility we enjoyed while also earning the income we needed?

I didn't really want to give up the freedom I'd come to accept as our reality. I was also desperate to make something happen. Then, just like that, all three of the jobs that had been presented to me were gone.

That's when I decided that no person, organization, or corporation would ever own my future again. I was not going to dust myself off and get back in the game. I was walking away. You could say I was taking my ball and going back to the garage.

During those dark days in the garage, even though the job I wanted never came, in my heart I went there. I wanted a job. I wanted the perceived security and status that comes with a job. When those three jobs slipped through my fingers, it was a wake-up call. Any job would be the same. Someone else would own my future.

◆

WHAT MAKES A CHOICE EASY?

Most people in my life -- pretty much everyone except for my wife and her family -- thought I was crazy a few years earlier when I had resigned from what many would have considered to be a dream job. I was twenty-seven years old and not only do I suspect that at the time I was making more money than any of my collegiate classmates, but I also had a tremendous amount of latitude in my position. My job afforded me opportunities to travel and to meet amazing people.

By way of my job, I enjoyed status in my community and in certain circles when I traveled.

And then I quit all that to buy a cafe.

I felt I had to quit because my passion for the job just wasn't there anymore. Sticking around just to collect a paycheck twice a month didn't seem right. I became convinced that if I stayed I would become a shell of a man.

My decision seemed maniacal to some, but for me it was an obvious decision. In fact, for me, there was almost no "choice" involved. Some choices seem obvious because they flow from values that we operate from unconsciously. I clearly value the idea of following my heart more than I do the idea of financial security. Therefore, while the question of financial security came up in my deliberations with regard to quitting my job, those questions took a back seat to questions of the heart.

I quit my job and worked on closing the deal to purchase the cafe. I had a vision to turn that cafe around and make it a model we could duplicate in other locations. Getting the deal done was a lot of work and there were many moving parts. We negotiated for months with the sellers and finally submitted our final, standing-on-our-tiptoes offer. Then, at the 11th hour, an all-cash offer came in from another buyer, wiping away all of our efforts.

Our dream of owning that cafe was over, but I dusted myself off. The way my mind works, I can spend endless hours working toward one vision for my life that I really want, and if it doesn't work out, I'll switch gears and get to work on another totally different, yet still totally exciting adventure.

That's what happened when we lost the cafe. I picked myself up and began building a consulting firm. It wasn't long before I was making as much money as I had made at the Reagan Ranch. Quickly, I began envisioning signing lots more clients and making lots more money. I'd hire an assistant and a few associates and open an office in a charming little stucco building with Spanish tiles in downtown Santa Barbara.

Then the Great Recession lingered and I started losing clients. Not deterred, I cashed out my retirement and mounted a campaign for Congress. Some of my critics called it a career move. If it was a career move, it was the worst career move in the history of careers! I didn't run for Congress as a career move; I felt compelled to run. In my heart, there was no getting away from it. I was either going to run away from what I felt I needed to do, or I was going to run for Congress.

After I lost, I had absolutely no idea what we were going to do next.

There are decisions we make in life that really matter, like dealing with issues of faith or choosing who we'll marry. While I struggled for a long time with issues of faith and in one way or another continue to do so, once I settle on certain things, making ultimate decisions regarding my faith was easy.

Like just about everyone else, I also struggled with relationships. Once I met Monica, though, there was never any doubt in my mind that we were going to get married. I never agonized or asked, "how do I know if she's the one?" because it was perfectly clear to me that she was.

My decision to quit my job at the Reagan Ranch was hard. Even though it seems obvious to me now, I did a lot of wrestling with myself as I deliberated what to do.

There were two big decisions I made in my path to unWorking.

First, I made the decision to quit my job.

Later, sitting in that garage and sensing my wife's hesitancy about getting another job, I made the decision to no longer give the best of my life to someone else and to abandon the idea of simply trading my time for money.

Quitting my job at the Reagan Ranch set my life on a path I never expected - good, bad and ugly. I've made some missteps along the way. I've lived a richer and fuller life, but it's been hard. It's also hurt. It hurt when I felt abandoned by my friends. It hurt having my ego take such tremendous blows. It hurt having people say, "I told you so."

The second decision, which you could call my decision to "stay quit," in many ways, was a decision not to change my mind about my first decision. While I was waiting on those three phone calls regarding those three jobs, I longed for escape. I teetered on the edge of retreat from that first decision. At the time, I would have loved for one of those job offers to have actually come through. I wonder what the conversations with my wife would have been like if we had been staring at an actual offer. For whatever reason, the offers never came and those conversations never happened.

It's hard to think about re-inventing your life when you are settled into the routines and comforts of your "normal" life. It was easier for me to think about re-inventing my life while sitting in my in-laws garage than it is for a Netflix executive to re-think his life while living in what I'm sure is a beautiful home in Silicon Valley and taking ski vacations at the Ritz Carlton. Those comforts, along with the joy and satisfaction of building a company that provides a service to millions of people, make it easy for one to settle.

But why did Mr. Netflix say he wanted to live a life like mine?

The answer is that most people don't know what they really want in life.

What about you?

Do you know what you want in life?

The author of the Harry Potter series, JK Rowling, said, "Rock bottom became the solid foundation from which I re-built my life."

Losing everything was the best thing that ever happened to me. It made me realize that losing everything isn't all that bad. I was forever freed from the fear of failure. I have been freed from the things I used to clutter my life with that I thought would make me happy. Rebuilding from nothing, I was given the opportunity to build from design.

Living in your in-laws garage doesn't have to be a bad thing.

The Big Take-Aways

Do not fear failure. Figure out what you want and even if things don't work out initially, that doesn't mean you aren't making progress. Embrace the idea of failing forward. Sometimes, when we face a string of failures in pursuit of what we want we are tempted to turn back, but "making progress" in the wrong direction is a pretty sad definition of success.

Money and things can actually cloud our vision when it comes to understanding what makes us happy. When my wife and I lost everything, we realized how much of our identity and relationships were wrapped up in my profession and status. We were embarrassed to not be living up to the image of ourselves we had created. Finally, when all ego was stripped away, we were able to rebuild by design.

The big take-away here is that losing everything rocks! If you can overcome the fear of failure, the whole world will be opened up to you.

Action Steps

1. Make a list of some of the underlying values in your life that make some decisions "no-brainers."

2. Think about a time in your life when something you really wanted didn't work out. How did you react? Did you quickly get excited about a new plan or did you cower back in fear?

3. What would you do today if you lost your job and I told you that you couldn't just go get another one?

4. Make a list of the things you are most afraid of losing. I'm not talking about your partner or your kids. I'm talking about money, security, status. Things you've built. Don't just think about this. Write them down. Then begin to envision how life could actually be exciting if you lost those things.

"The ability to set goals and to make plans for their accomplishment is the master skill of success. Developing this skill will do more to ensure your success than anything else you could ever do."

Brian Tracey

CHAPTER 3

Casting a vision for your future

Where there is no vision, the people will perish.

It's a line from the Book of Proverbs, written by Solomon, whom the Bible says was the wisest man to ever live.

Perish.

Think about that word for a minute.

Where there is no vision, people perish.

Not linger. Not waver. Not be less productive or less joyful. Not lack meaning or purpose. Not aimless or lacking cause.

Perish.

Which is to say, without a vision, we die.

When I was wrestling with whether or not to quit my job at the Reagan Ranch, I came to the conclusion that if I were to stay, I would be a shell of a man. I felt like I would be dead on the inside. I think that's because if I had stayed I would have had no true and pure vision for my life.

I'll admit that in the years since I quit I've had moments -- though not seasons -- of depression. There have been dark days. But depression, even in my lowest of times, has never defined my life because of vision. Even as we were moving into the in-laws garage, I felt excited about the future because I had a vision, albeit a foggy one, for the future.

Shortly after we settled into our garage-home, I had a poster board printed with pictures of the ski slopes in Lake Tahoe and other places around the world. That was my vision for the future and I wanted to be visually reminded of it every day that we called that garage our home.

Do you wake up in the morning and go to work because that's just what you do? Do you even know what you are working toward?

Until you have a damn good idea of what you want, stop working. Travel. Ski. Think. Take a sabbatical or a gap year. Give your mind and spirit some time to figure things out.

I'm not saying you need to have everything figured out. I didn't have everything figured out in terms of our vision when we were in the garage. Far from it. I'm not asking you to develop a vision for the future that's detailed and set in stone. I am saying that it would be a better use of your time to stop and really think about what you want in life than to continue mindlessly spinning your wheels.

After my campaign for congress ended, it was time to figure out what to do next. In chapter two, I shared about the three elusive jobs I was contacted about, but I also interviewed with a few companies in Santa Barbara where we were living.

I was offered a job with a company that was a little over a year old. I'd make a decent base salary but would also get commissions and some equity in the company. My friend in Montecito, the one with the beautiful home I mentioned earlier, gave me some of the best advise I've ever received in my life as I was considering this job.

He asked me if I really believed in the company. Did I buy into their vision? Did I think this company was *special?*

He said, "Clark, if you really believe this company is going places, go for it, because you'll work really hard for a few years but the payoff could be tremendous. If you don't believe in it though, you should do something else because you'll work too hard and the payoff will never be there." I turned down the job because I didn't believe the company was going places.

Still, how could I turn down a job?

The three jobs around the country that I'd actually been interested in didn't work out. For whatever reason, each just fell off the map. Now I had a job opportunity right in my back yard. My family was living in a garage. How could I responsibly turn down a job that lots of people would say was a great opportunity?

I didn't believe the company was going places, but more importantly, I turned it down because my wife hesitated. She understood before I did that taking a job wasn't going to help us get what we wanted in life.

Instead, I became a rep for a credit card processing company, hardly a job I was passionate about, but it was work that would accomplish two important goals. First, although a sales cycle would require me to be present, once a client was obtained that relationship could be maintained whether I was in Santa Barbara or anywhere else in the world. This was important to us for our goal to be location independent and have the freedom to travel. Second, although I'd make very little money initially, over time I could build up a passive, residual stream of income. Passive. Residual. Income. Those three words were like music to my ears.

I worked hard to build a client base and I went cold calling. Every day I'd pick a neighborhood in Santa Barbara and I'd go door to door, visiting one business after another after another. There was a lot of rejection, but I found a client here and a client there. If only more people had given me the time of day. I saved one client more than $20,000 a year on their credit card processing fees.

When I wasn't pounding the pavement trying to add new accounts, Monica and I were talking vision. What did we want our life to look like?

After five months in the in-laws garage, we headed to Monica's grandfather's cabin in Tahoe for the winter. His home would give our family a little space. We'd ski and I'd test the South Lake Tahoe market to see if it would be a good place to continue growing my portfolio of credit card merchant clients.

I'll always remember that winter in Tahoe as a special season in our lives. Our life was simple. All we did was spend time together, work on adding new credit card processing accounts and ski. That was it. We didn't have television and we had not started blogging or building our online empire yet. In the evenings, after the kids were in bed, Monica and I would sit by the fire and talk. We talked for hours and hours. We were asking questions and figuring things out. We were fleshing out our vision for the future.

Settling on a vision for the future is important because once you settle on a vision, you can stop wasting your time doing things that aren't helping you achieve a life of your design and focus only on those things that do.

A vision for the future will help sustain you when life gets hard or things aren't going your way. Having a vision and working to achieve that vision brings hope into your life. Hope is a powerful thing. Because I had hope, even when I was living in the in-laws garage I could remain optimistic about the future.

That first winter in Tahoe Monica and I talked about what we wanted. We talked about having a beautiful home in Tahoe or a beautiful home in Santa Barbara. We talked about having a home in both places and splitting our time between the two. We talked about travel. We talked about how we engage with our friends and our community. We talked about our kids and what we wanted life to look like as they grow, as well as what we hoped life would look like once they reach adulthood.

We talked about money. We talked about how much money we would need to make in order to do the things that were important to us. We talked about what work would have to look like for us in order for us to do the things we wanted to do not just when we reach "retirement age," but all along the way.

We talked and we talked and we talked.

You need a vision for the future. To develop a vision for the future, you've got to talk.

If you're married, your spouse is your partner. The word "partner" is one of my favorite terms I use to refer to my wife because she truly is my partner in every sense of the word. If you're not married or in a committed relationship, find a friend who wants to develop a vision for his or her life and start talking with that person. Together you can help one another define your vision of what you want life to look like.

Talk it out.

Don't be afraid of making statements that contradict one another. Either you'll figure out a way to reconcile those seemingly contradicting statements, or you'll eventually make a decision that you value one thing over another.

Finally, realize that am I not suggesting you need a detailed, set-in-stone vision before you go to work. I'm not sure I believe in having a set-in-stone vision for my own life.

Over the past few years, our vision for the future has gone through minor transitions. We adjust, but we're moving in a general direction now. We have a vision. What life actually looks like as we pass different milestones on our path to achieve that vision can change. We've got our vision, but looking from afar it is hard to see variations in the landscape.

We're not roaming aimlessly. We're not perishing. We're not dying. We're living intentionally and trying to ensure that the way we live actually lines up with what we value most.

◆

AM I LAZY?

Sometimes, because I refuse to "get a job," people accuse me of being lazy. It's not that I'm lazy, it's just that I'm not going to give my life for something that is not of the utmost importance to me.

Several years ago, after I had left my job at the Reagan Ranch but before I had really thought about reinventing my life, I was talking with a gentleman I'd know for quite a while and become relatively close to. This man had achieved substantial financial success, had enjoyed a happy marriage, and had great kids with whom he had great relationships. His life at that moment, though, was marked by deep sadness. Within the first year of his retirement, his wife had been diagnosed with Alzheimer's disease.

"I wish I had retired two years sooner," he said to me.

I remember thinking at the time, "two years?"

"Are you kidding me? Two years!"

If I were in that situation, I'd be thinking, "I wish I had lived my whole life differently." Two years is a pittance. He wished he had retired two years earlier so he could have enjoyed those years with his wife before the disease started taking her away? His statement made absolutely no sense to me. Two years seemed like so little, and I had this feeling that I could work my whole life toward a goal and reach the finish line and learn that my wife or me were sick. Or I could not reach the finish line at all.

I don't want to wake up someday and wonder what the hell happened to my life. I don't want to give the best years of my life to someone else.

◆

THE CASE FOR WORK

I actually enjoy work. I find I'm happiest in life when I am able to spend time with my family, when I am doing recreational activities I enjoy and when I am simultaneously engaged in work that I am passionate about.

In 2009, when our family went on the six month road trip across the United States I referred to earlier, I left with a pretty decent portfolio of consulting work. This was during the Great Recession and that quickly changed. A few months into the trip I had very little work. The last few months of the trip I had almost no work. And even though we were traveling across the country and constantly experiencing new things, I felt like there was something missing from my life. I learned then that a life of leisure is not a worthy goal. I want to do something. I want to work. I want to create something beautiful. For me, that does not equate to getting a job.

I'm trying to take a more direct path to happiness. Rather than making as much money as possible and then buying all the happiness money can buy, I'm doing the things that make me most happy and then figuring out a way to make the money I need to sustain a life of my own design. I'm cutting out the middle man.

As you develop your own vision for a life of your own design, take the most direct path to get there. Don't tell yourself that your goal in life is to live at the beach or in the mountains, and then spend 30 or 40 years doing something else, when you could move to the beach or the mountains today.

Whatever you want to do, figure out a way to do it.

Now.

Do it before your spouse gets the diagnosis that makes your heart sink. Do it before your company goes belly-up when you're just a few months away from your retirement. Do it before your kids are out of the house and have entered the same rat race that you're in now.

Don't wait.

Do it.

Now.

Over time, Monica and I figured out that our vision was to work less, live more, and travel the world as a family. What that actually looks like in different seasons of our life can vary.

Home for us now is beautiful Lake Tahoe. Named North America's most beautiful lake in 2012 by USA Today, Lake Tahoe is paradise. We average more than 400 inches of snow annually, which is great for our ski habit, but we also enjoy 300 days of sunshine a year. Lake Tahoe's beaches in the summer are like a tropical paradise, even if the water is a bit cold. If we want to change things up we can hike to one of the hundreds of alpine lakes in the area. We can bike, swim, paddle-board. It's a year-round playground. I love Tahoe and I call Tahoe home not because I have a job there, but because I *want* to live in Tahoe.

"As it lay there with the shadows of the mountains brilliantly photographed upon its still surface I thought it must surely be the fairest picture the whole earth affords," Mark Twain wrote of his first impressions of Lake Tahoe. He continued, "The air up there in the clouds is very pure and fine, bracing and delicious. And why shouldn't it be? -- it is the same the angels breathe."

When we came to Tahoe we didn't realize that we'd stay. We're not the first people this has happened to; Tahoe casts a spell. We were in the family cabin initially, and thought we were just going to be in Tahoe until we were ready to set off on a round-the-world trip. Tahoe captivated us, though, and while we once thought that we would set off to "travel forever," we eventually changed that to the idea that we were preparing to go on a two year trip around the world so that we could come back to Tahoe after a specific amount of time.

Through our blog FamilyTrek.org we'd met lots of families who were on similar traveling adventures and we wanted to throw our hat in the ring. Over time we decided that maybe indefinite travel wasn't for us, at least not right now. We valued having a home base and we valued traveling adventures. How would we reconcile these two different things?

In 2012 we sub-let the house we were renting in Tahoe while we traveled in Central America. In 2014, we actually moved out of our house and became "homeless." The possessions we did not sell were put into storage to free ourselves up to travel in Thailand for three months. Presently, our plan is to travel most of the year and then get a vacation rental each winter in Tahoe. That will probably change at some point and we have some ideas about that, but can't say for sure.

I think that through the course of our lives we'll probably take an all the above approach. We'll likely set off on periods of open-ended travel. We'll put our stuff in storage and rent a house in Peru or some other far corner of the world for six months. We'll enjoy our home base of Tahoe.

Working less, living more and traveling the world as a family is our vision in a very broad sense, what that actually looks like can change.

◆

PROTESTANT WORK ETHIC?

I've spoken about my realization that a life of leisure was not a worthy goal and how I find joy and satisfaction in my work, but I'm just not sure about that whole "Protestant work ethic" thing being an ethic at all.

Americans work longer hours, take less vacation time and retire later in life than any other people in the world. In a brilliant piece titled 10 Things Most Americans don't know about America, author Mark Manson says that one problem Americans have is that we mistake comfort for happiness. "The United States," he writes, "is a country built on the exaltation of economic growth and personal ingenuity." Comfort sells. Work harder, get more stuff, be more comfortable.

Manson defines being wealthy as "having the freedom to maximize one's life experiences." By that definition, he writes, "despite the average American having more material wealth than citizens of most other countries (more cars, bigger houses, nicer televisions), their overall quality of life suffers... American people on average work more hours with less vacation, spend more time commuting every day, and are saddled with over $10,000 of debt. That's a lot of time spent working and buying crap and little time or disposable income for relationships, activities or new experiences."

The United States is the only industrialized country in the world with no mandated annual vacation time. According to the International Labour Organization, "Americans work 137 more hours per year than Japanese workers, 260 more hours per year than British workers and 499 more hours per year than French workers."

Even if you manage to get a job in the United States where your employer provides vacation time, there's often tremendous pressure to not take your vacation time. Taking your vacation time could cause you to be passed over for a promotion. When I worked at the Reagan Ranch, we were discouraged from taking vacation time and instead encouraged to cash in our vacation time for a vacation pay check at the end of each year. The message? Don't take your vacation. Work harder. Take money and buy more stuff to get more "comfortable."

I want to live more! I want to ski and go to the beach and hike and bike and paddle-board. I want to travel and see the world. I want to eat good food and drink good wine. I want to go to parties and host parties. I want to play with my kids and I want to be, along with my wife, the primary educator of my kids. I want to live epicly!

We also want to travel and see the world. Will we travel for a year? Indefinitely? Move to South America for six months? Spend winters in Tahoe and then travel six months out of every year? Anything can happen since we're not tied to a traditional job!

As you consider your own lifestyle design, it may be hard for you to figure out exactly what you want to do.

That's okay.

I'm working toward fulfilling my desire to travel in whatever form I choose. I've discovered that for me it's all about achieving and maintaining the freedom to have choices.

We have a general idea, a direction we are going, but it's not precise and it's not set in stone.

In order to achieve and maintain our freedom of choice, my wife and I have three tenets in our life:

1. Get out of debt.

2. Keep our expenses low.

3. Only take on work that is location independent

◆

GET OUT OF DEBT

Debt is an anchor and when Monica and I began working to achieve a life of our own design we had a lot of debt. We had a big anchor holding us back. It was hard to live a life of our own design because we were still paying for the aimless life we once lived.

◆

KEEP OUR EXPENSES LOW

When I quit my job at the Reagan Ranch, our household expenses at the time -- just paying the mortgage, utilities, association dues and insurance -- totaled $7,000 a month. Car payments, car insurance, gas, food, credit card payments, and payments on our student loans easily pushed that number over $11,000 a month. Every month we had to come up with $11,000, just to cover our basic expenses before we'd saved a penny or spent a penny on leisure.

With such high expenses, we weren't nimble at all. Now, we obsess over keeping our monthly expenses low. We don't have cable TV or a home phone. During the three years that we were in a long-term housing situation in Tahoe, I gathered, split and stacked my own firewood to heat our home. We ditched high price cell phone carriers. We avoid taking on anything that includes a monthly payment like the plague.

By keeping our expenses low, we're not facing financial ruin if something doesn't work out the way we think it's going to. It also means that the little bits of money we make here and there through our patchwork income approach are a big deal. If I made $200 doing something when my monthly expenses were $11,000 a month, that $200 represented less than 2 percent of my monthly expenses. Now, that same amount of money would represent a much greaters perentage because our monthly, ongoing obligations are so low.

◆

ONLY TAKE ON WORK THAT IS LOCATION INDEPENDENT

I said earlier that if my goal is to ski 60 days a year and also to be a present husband and father, it does not matter how much money I make; if I have to be present at a job five days a week or more for 40 hours a week or more, accepting that job would be counterproductive to my goals.

If I want to be free to travel the world -- whether that's for a season of open-ended travel, moving to a new place every few years, or traveling six months a year -- taking on work that requires me to be in any one place is counterproductive to my goal.

If we are in a particular place and want to take on some work while we're there, no problem. In terms of long-term commitments, though, one question we ask ourselves before we take on work is this: *"Could we do this from anywhere in the world?"* If the answer is no, we know it's not the right kind of work for us. The money may sound nice, but for us it's the wrong kind of money.

Our three tenets -- no debt, keeping expenses low, and only taking location independent work -- are all crucial to our lifestyle design. They may not be true, however, in your lifestyle design. Living in Lake Tahoe, I have met many people who have arranged their lives to live in the mountains who aren't so concerned with location independence. One of my friends from college who lives in Indiana dreamed of living on a farm with a picturesque barn. She and her husband saved their pennies and sacrificed other momentary wants in order to get what they ultimately wanted. I've seen the pictures and their barn is right out of a storybook, and today she and her family live mainly off their own land, growing their own food and raising their own animals.

In establishing your own tenants for achieving and sustaining the life of your dreams, the important thing is to give yourself a framework that will allow you to achieve your goals broadly, acknowledging that what you want long-term may subtly change.

Figuring out your vision is directly related to your goals for what you want life to look like. Establishing your tenets is how you'll get there. If you can look at your tenets and say, "If I do these things, I'll be free to live the life of my dreams," then you are on the right track.

The Big Take-Aways

In many ways, this chapter is designed to get you thinking about your life the way you would prepare to write a business plan. After I left my job at the Reagan Ranch, I wrote lots of business plans for myself and others. Many of the questions Monica and I wrestled with as we went through the process of defining what we wanted in life are the types of questions you need to grapple with when writing a business plan.

If you take nothing else from this chapter, I hope it would be my assertion that you need to stop spinning your wheels. Don't just keep trudging along. Give yourself time and space to figure out what you want. Doing nothing but thinking about what you want life to look like is far more productive than doing lots of things that don't help you get to where you ultimately want to be. If you're afraid of doing nothing, don't worry. On their death-bed people never say they wish they had worked more. Most people hear that and think there's nothing they can do about it. But you can.

Having a vision for your future will help you do the hard work when the time for working comes. But you've got to have the vision. It's not enough to say, "let's cut our expenses and save money, then we'll be free to do what we want when we discover it...." That's not enough motivation. Your vision should make you salivate.

Finally, find someone who will support you. You need someone who will talk through these issues with you and help you flesh out your vision and ask you hard questions. Ideally, this would be someone who knows you well enough to know if you're blowing smoke. And this person certainly needs to be someone who will root for you!

Action Steps

Write a business plan for your life. It doesn't have to be as detailed as you might make it if you were taking it to potential investors, but here are some good things to think about:

1. Who are you? What is your life mission? What are your goals and objectives? What are your values? What is your vision? Sit down with a piece of paper and begin formulating your thoughts about these things.

2. A business plan would consider the overall business environment. If you were to write out a life plan, you may want to consider the environment you're trying to achieve all of this in. For example, Monica and I are working toward location independence via patchwork income. We felt this was a good decision not just because it lined up with our values, but we also believe that this approach to life is increasingly the norm in the emerging

world, thus we'll be set up for success as our approach increasingly becomes the norm.

3. Think about your competitive advantages. Why are you the best person in the world to live the life you envision?

4. Make a list of where you want to be a year from now, two years from now, and five years from now in terms of living a life of your own design. What are some big things that need to happen? Do you need to pay down debt? Start the project that's been on your mind for years? Start building up location independent income? What needs to happen for you to live a life of your own design. Make a list of those things.

"Many people die with their music still in them. Why is this so? Too often it is because they are always getting ready to live. Before they know it, time runs out."

Oliver Wendell Holmes

CHAPTER 4

Living in the Now

In the last chapter I wrote about the man I knew whose wife was diagnosed with Alzheimer's disease less than a year after he retired. He regretted not retiring sooner, wishing that he would have had a few extra years with her before the disease slowly began to take her away.

Two years?

Really, that's it?

He wishes he would have had two years?

What about the rest of the years?

I don't want to wake up at the age of 65 and wonder what happened to my life. I don't want to work my butt off now, while my kids are young, so that I can retire when they are no longer around. I don't want to wait to travel to see the world with my wife until we're old and can't get around like we can now. I don't want to wait until I'm 60 years old to ski 60 days a year.

I don't want to wake up at 65 and wonder what the hell happened to my life.

I don't want to wake up at 40 wondering that either.

◆

CARPE DIEM

It took close to a year of talking -- from the time that we moved into the in-laws garage to the time we moved out of grandpa's cabin and rented our own place in Tahoe -- before we began to understand what we really wanted in life.

Simple.

Family.

Travel.

Skiing.

Beach days.

Less Debt.

Fewer obligations.

Less pressure.

More time for ourselves.

Work we are passionate about.

For us, the Great Recession had been the Great Reorientation.

I've talked about how I don't want to give the best years of my life to someone else. I've talked about developing a vision for the future and creating a life of your own design.

But what about now?

Monica and I developed a vision to work less, live more, and travel the world as a family.

When would we begin doing that?

We began immediately.

We didn't say, "Let's work really hard for two years and save a bunch of money, and then we'll work less, live more, and travel the world as a family."

We didn't say, "Let's work really hard and pay off all of our debt, and then we'll work less, live more, and travel the world as a family."

We didn't say, "Let's build up our location independent income, and then we'll work less, live more, and travel the world as a family."

We began immediately.

Because tomorrow isn't guaranteed.

◆

THE GIFT OF TODAY

On our first date, Monica and I fell off a 90-foot cliff.

We'd been seeing a lot of each other, but on this particular Sunday we spent the entire day together. I picked her up to go out for breakfast and it was after 11 o'clock when I started walking her out to her car from my house that night. At the time, I lived on the bluffs called the Mesa in Santa Barbara overlooking the Pacific Ocean. There was an overlook spot a block from my house where people often went to look out at the ocean. Not ready for the night to end, I suggested we head over.

We had the "defining the relationship" talk. It was after midnight at this point but we decided to walk out near the edge of the bluffs to really take in the ocean views before calling it a night.

We didn't know it, but the ground beneath our feet was badly eroded. My last memory was realizing we were going to fall. Monica remembers the fall and remembers thinking, "this is it... this is how I am going to die."

It was after midnight when we fell, so nobody was around to see what had happened or to help us. More than two hours later, I was found back at street level. Although I have no recollection of doing this, I crawled the equivalent of four blocks down the beach and up 300 steps to get back up to the top of the bluffs.

Monica was unconscious for most of the time, but for more than two hours, she had been laying on the beach and unable to move. At first she was afraid she was paralyzed, but she was able to move her feet. She could not roll over off of her stomach or get up. Back at the top of the bluffs, I waved down a car for help. This is the first thing I remember after realizing we were going to fall. I don't even remember the car stopping. I only remember trying to wave it down. The car did stop, though, and the driver called 911. I remember the paramedics being there and not knowing where I was, how I had gotten there, or what happened to me.

In the ambulance I had a flashback. That's when they went to go find Monica. Although she remembered the fall, she thought that it must have been a dream. Because she was laying on the beach, she reasoned she must have been shipwrecked! When the surgical team found her one of them said to her, "don't worry, your boyfriend is alright," to which Monica replied, "did he really say that he was my boyfriend?"

Once I remembered what had happened and that Monica was down at the bottom of the bluffs, I was... I don't know the word. I thought Monica was dead. I was still so out of it; still in and out of consciousness. I was terrified though. I kept asking if they had found her and they kept telling me they had not. Finally, they told me they had found her and that she was okay.

I didn't believe them. By this time, doctors were working on putting my head back together -- I had a fractured skull and had been scalped. I thought that they were only telling me this because they knew I'd lose it if they told me the truth.

Finally, Monica arrived at the hospital. We were in neighboring rooms in the ER separated by a window and curtains. Nurses propped both of us up and opened the curtains so we could wave at each other.

Monica had three fractures in her pelvis and we both spent a few days in the hospital. This, by the way, was an interesting way to announce to the world that we were dating.

Each year on the anniversary of "The Fall" we hold a Celebration of Life Party. It's an opportunity each year for us to bring ourselves back to the idea that life is a precious and fleeting gift and that were it not for the grace of God, that night could have been it. All my life I've lived with the sense that life is both short and fragile. I remember feeling that way as a seventeen year-old high school kid. Falling off a cliff only accentuated those feelings.

Tomorrow is not guaranteed, so it's not just about where I'm going, it's about where I am right now. What if Monica and I decided to put our noses to the grindstone for a couple of years and something terrible happened to one of us or one of our kids?

Do you think we'd regret our decision?

I'm really excited about what the future looks like for our family. I'm equally excited about the present. I could spend the next 40 years of my life working my butt off, doing the respectable thing that meets society's expectations of what makes a good and upstanding citizen, and there's still no guarantee that it will all work out. The best laid plans of mice and men are but the best laid plans of mice and men.

The Great Recession should have taught all of us this. Why hasn't the Great Recession been a Great Reorientation for more people?

At the onset of The Great Recession, I remember talking to men who had a look of fear in their eyes. They'd gone down this path for 30 or 40 years and suddenly the rug was being pulled out from under them. I knew more than one person who took their own life during the financial crisis and Great Recession.

These men had given away decades of their lives. Now, they were finding that the reward was a mirage.

"Here's something that happens all the time and makes no sense at all," Solomon the wise wrote in the Book of Ecclesiastes. "Good people get what's coming to the wicked, and bad people get what's coming to the good. I tell you, this makes no sense. It's smoke. So, I'm all for just going ahead and having a good time—the best possible. The only earthly good men and women can look forward to is to eat and drink well and have a good time—compensation for the struggle for survival these few years God gives us on earth."

Eat, drink, and be merry.

Live epicly now.

◆

START HOARDING

I have a vision for the future while living in the present. As our family prepared for three months in Thailand we were really, really excited. We're excited for future travels in Central America and North American road-trips and to every far corner of the world. If we've not been there yet, trust me, it's on the list! But our travels are not escapes. I'm not trying to escape from anything. My life in Lake Tahoe is awesome. When I'm at the top of Heavenly Mountain getting ready to ski down a run with the most stunning views of Lake Tahoe in front of me, I am happy. No need to escape from that.

I don't want to take an epic trip. I want to have an epic life.

What would living epicly look like for you?

For me, it's about being free. It's about being able to be around the house with my kids without having to go to an office. It's being able to ski 60 days a year, and having 60 more beach days, either in Lake Tahoe or some other beach in some far corner of the world. It's hiking, cycling, and all sorts of outdoor adventures. It's having the freedom to travel without having to ask someone for time off. For me, living epicly is spending six weeks in Central America, constantly touring around California and spending three months in Thailand. It's having a plan to work today, but realizing that my daughter is sick and she just wants to cuddle and I can cuddle with her and I don't have to call anyone to ask for the day off. Or, it's planning to work today, but waking up and realizing a foot of snow has fallen and I can push everything else aside for a powder day.

Living epicly is about being able to spend time with my family. It's about watching my kids grow up. Along with my wife, I want to be the primary facilitator of my kids' educations. I want to be able to eat three leisurely meals a day with my kids on a regular basis and then go play in the backyard or go on bike rides or go skiing together. I want to be able to spend most of the day, most every day, with my wife.

Living epicly is also the decision to throw myself into work projects that excite me. Sure, there's work I do that doesn't excite me. I've got to admit, I'm not all that excited about being a credit card processing rep. It's work and it brings in some good money on terms that fit our lifestyle. I don't think the work I do as a credit card processing rep is *great* work. I think it's competent. My clients get very competitive pricing and excellent customer service. I'm not sure there's anything great about it though, and I want to do great work.

Steve Jobs said the only way to do really great work is to do work that we really love. Maybe that's just Kool-Aid, but I drank it. I want to do great work, therefore I want to do work that I love.

These are all things I can do right now. I don't need to have all of my debt paid off or have a certain amount of money in savings. I can do it right now. While society tells us to buy more stuff to be more comfortable, I'm hoarding experiences instead.

How can you live epicly right now?

It's great to have a vision for the future. If you don't have one, get one. Start talking with your spouse or a friend. But in the meantime, enjoy life now, because tomorrow isn't guaranteed.

The Big Take-Aways

Do you survive 51 weeks a year and count down the days until you can take that one week vacation? Are you obsessed with when you can retire? If so, then something needs to change! Life is too short and too precious to not spend it doing things that you love. There can be so much more to life than just surviving. There's so much more than just trudging though. What's more? I believe you have something to offer the world that only you can give, and when you give it you make the whole world more rich and more beautiful.

Howard Thurman once wrote, "Don't ask yourself what the world needs. Ask yourself what makes you come alive and go do that, because what the world needs is people who come alive."

Live epicly now. Don't put it off. Don't merely sustain yourself with the hope of a better tomorrow. Your life can be great, it can be epic, now.

Action Steps

1. If tomorrow you were admitted to the hospital and you were told that you had a very short time to live, what would you regret? I know people say we should not live with regrets, but think about this for a moment. What would you have done differently? What can you learn from this "regret?" How can you live differently now that you know about this "regret?"

2. What kind of work do you find meaningful? What makes you feel alive? Are you doing work today that you love? Do you have side projects? Side projects are a great way to discover what you love. Try lots of different things. Maybe you know what you love but you can't make enough money doing it, but that's no reason to not start doing something you love on the side. Over time, maybe your side project will grow, or maybe it will lead you to a new discovery.

3. What do you value in life? Work is going to comprise a significant part of your life, so you should do something you love. What do you want to do with the rest of your time, though? For me it's skiing, traveling, and being with my family. What is it for you? What do you value? Arrange your life around those things.

"Remember the compliments you receive, forget the insults;

If you succeed in doing this, tell me how."

Mary Schmich,
"Wear Sunscreen"

CHAPTER 5

It's Hard to Find a Friend

Everything I've shared with you up to this point is pretty easy:

1. Figure out what you want.

2. Go after it.

3. Have fun along the way.

What I am about to share with you is really hard. I've got to admit, I didn't do so well at this part of the whole life re-invention thing.

◆

A COLD AND BROKEN HALLELUJAH

I felt terribly alone living in the in-laws garage. My relationship with my wife and kids was strong, but everyone else was gone. Although Monica and I were full of hope regarding our future, I also struggled with waves of depression.

I'd sit in the garage at night reading and drinking cheap whiskey, wondering what happened to everyone. I felt like I had lots of friends when I was a big shot. I used to be able to call anyone and go to any restaurant I wanted in Santa Barbara. Monica and I would host parties at our house and there would be so many people we could hardly fit them all in.

Where were all those people now?

I remember Monica asking me once as she was getting ready to go into the house for the night, "Is there someone you want to call to see if you can get together?"

"Who am I going to call?" was my reply.

Looking back, it's still sad to me that nobody really reached out to us considering everything we were going through. I hope that because of the experiences we went though that if I ever sense someone in my life is going through something similar that I will run to them. Yet I can't just blame my absent friends. I also have myself to blame.

My hope is that I can help you avoid some of the relationship strains I experienced as a result of our lifestyle changes. The best advice I can give you is to be open and honest, which is pretty much the opposite of what I did.

I became a fake.

◆

TRANSPARENT

There were many reasons my wife and I decided to move from Santa Barbara and make Lake Tahoe our home. For starters, the skiing is a whole lot better in Tahoe than it is in Santa Barbara. We also fell in love with the natural beauty of Tahoe and the raw and rocky forests peppered with its Jeffrey Pines.

After we moved and began to make friends we realized another benefit:

no expectations.

Having attained a level of success in Santa Barbara, I wanted to maintain the appearance that everything was great. I worked really hard to make sure nobody ever knew how much we were struggling. When I ran for Congress, we were sitting on a house of cards. When my campaign ended, that house of cards collapsed. I was determined to maintain appearances, so very few people knew what we were going through. Many of my friends in Santa Barbara did not know I'd even lived in my in-laws garage until several months after we moved to Lake Tahoe and I wrote a blog post about the experience that I shared on my Facebook page.

When we moved to Tahoe, I was completely broken and I was tired of trying to keep up appearances, so I became completely transparent. No pretension. No ego.

My hope is that this book is inspiring some change in your life. It's exciting to think about living a life of your own design. I think it'd be irresponsible of me to only tell you about the exciting parts. The strain your change in lifestyle could put on your relationships with friends and family is potentially one of the hardest.

So why didn't I talk openly with my friends?

What Monica and I went through was transformative, although difficult to communicate with those whose lives went on as before. In many ways, while we were still living in Santa Barbara we couldn't put our fingers on exactly what we were going through.

I want to share what I regret because I'd like to help you avoid making a similar mistake.

For me, when I lived in Santa Barbara, getting together with a friend almost always meant going for drinks at some cool spot. Food and cigars usually followed. It was hard to go anywhere with my friends -- at least the way I had come to understand going anywhere with my friends -- without dropping some serious dough.

When we were living in the garage, I had no money. My bank account probably had 33 cents in it, if it was not overdrawn. I probably could have found a few coins in my car. That's it. There was no way I could afford to go and do all those things I was used to doing with my friends. I couldn't bring myself to admitting to my friends that I was broke. Not in the sense that, "I have the money but I am trying to watch things closely this month..." We're talking no money. None.

I was so embarrassed.

Looking back, I regret that I didn't tell my friends I couldn't afford to go.

I wish I would have called them up and suggested we go on a hike. And if they would have suggested drinks instead, I wish I would have just been honest. Some friendships would have probably faded over time. Some friendships really were built on little more than Grey Goose martinis and fine cigars and that's okay. The friendships that were built on something more substantial wouldn't have been dealt such tremendous blows.

A few years removed from Santa Barbara, I'm only now having some of those conversations with friends with whom I was once very close. Each of my friends have been excited to hear about the way I'd re-invented my life.

It's easy to share my life choices with my friends from where I'm sitting now -- in a position of relative success with a new lifestyle. *I* mean it's hard to argue with success. One of my friends, who happens to be quite affluent, told me that I was his hero because I'd figured out how to live like a millionaire without having a lot of money.

When I first moved into my in-laws garage, I was only at the beginning of my life re-invention; I was broke, ashamed, and embarrased. So I didn't call anyone, and, in most cases, they didn't call me. Those who did call weren't likely to get a return call from me.

As time went on, some of the choices my wife and I made and the things we wrote on our blog further drove away some of our friends and our family. Any change in lifestyle is going to meet with some resistance from your current lifestyle and the people you have shared that old lifestyle with. Your friends or extended family may view your choices as a judgment on them.

I want you to be prepared for this. I want to make sure you count this as a cost of any changes you're about to make in your life.

For me, the strains and the tension have been worth it. Looking back, I would have done some things differently along the way, but the benefits I get out of living and continuing to pursue a life of my own design outweigh any drawbacks. I believe I'm living a life that my Maker designed me to live. I believe that when anyone pursues that kind of life they'll find that the positive consequences far outweigh the negative consequences.

Do whatever you can to share what you're going through. Be more open and more available than I was. Challenge your friends to think about their own vision for the future and be excited for them as they lay out that vision, even if it's different from your vision for your life. Give them the grace you'd like them to give you. Your life is your life. Their life is their life.

◆

GOALS GONE STALE

A lot of people couldn't understand why in the world I'd want to make a change. The fact that I wanted a change when my life was so seemingly perfect perhaps made me look like an ass. From some people's perspective, I was throwing away a life they would have given anything for.

My life in Santa Barbara felt like lightyears away from my life in Indiana, where I had grown up. Cornfields were replaced by beaches. Meat and potatoes were replaced by oysters and tuna tartare and so many delicacies. I learned there were more spices than just salt and pepper. Conversations with friends in the laundry room of my dorm were replaced by conversations with cabinet secretaries or best-selling authors over a cocktail.

I didn't make as much money as a lot of my friends in Santa Barbara, but I was doing pretty darn well. There was more to it than the money, though. I was exactly where I had envisioned myself being when I was an 18 or 19 year old college student. Everything was going as planned.

There was only one problem.

I didn't want to be there anymore.

I was continually growing more disinterested in my work and the passion wasn't there anymore.

In the fall of 2007, a few months before I would quit my job at the Reagan Ranch, I traveled back to Indiana to visit my alma mater, Indiana Wesleyan University. I was there for meetings, but what I was really interested in doing was spending some time with old college friends who were now working at the university. One evening, I spent a few hours in the Williams Prayer Chapel. Afterward, I scribbled some notes in my journal while enjoying a latte at McConn Coffee Co. in the Student Center:

"I have this increasing sense that I am not where God wants me to be."

Three months later, I quit my job.

That's one of the prouder moments of my life.

Can you imagine writing that line -- "I have this increasing sense that I am not where God wants me to be" - and seven or ten years later being in the exact same place? I absolutely had to quit. I would have been dead if I stayed.

"Every man dies, not every man really lives."

That's William Wallace talking. It's the pinnacle moment in Braveheart. Quitting was my way of making the decision to live.

◆

YOU'VE GOT A FRIEND (AND THE HATERS)

I remember the first time I expressed to anyone other than my wife that I was considering quitting my job at the Reagan Ranch. My closest friends knew I had increasing interest in opportunities outside of my job, but the fact that I was thinking about quitting was big news.

Over the next weeks and months as I prepared to quit my job, I interacted with three friends. There were many voices in my life, but all can largely be categorized into the character of these three friends:

1. My friend who thought I was crazy.

2. My friend who thought I was awesome.

3. My friend who was mad at me.

I had a lot of friends who thought I was crazy. I had my dream job and twice a month my employer made a direct deposit of thousands of dollars into my bank account. Now I would have no guarantee that I'd make any money. All I had was an idea and the overwhelming sense that I had to do something different -- that I could not just "suck it up" and dutifully trudge through life.

Others thought I was awesome. They'd listen to me talk about how I was chasing my dream and say things like, "Man, I wish I had the courage to do that."

There were also some friends and family members who were mad at me. How could I turn my back on such a dream scenario? Some of these people viewed me as being irresponsible. Others, I have come to realize, were mad because they would no longer have a direct link to some of the cool opportunities my position afforded me.

I loved friend Number One. I take crazy as a compliment. Friend Number Two was fun to hang out and in a way these people were akin to someone throwing gasoline on a fire. But Friend Number Three? That's another story.

My dad was Friend Number Three.

My dad's dream was to be a politician, a statesman. I've seen the photos of him when he was 17 or 18 years old; American flag hanging and the banner reading, "To the Vandeventer White House Bid of 1992." And it just never worked out for him. When I was at the Reagan Ranch rubbing shoulders with the rich and powerful, my dad lived vicariously through me. When I was a candidate for United States Congress, my dad beamed with pride.

There are some men who relive glories of high school football through their kids. Nothing would please these men more than to see their boy end up being the star quarterback, landing a scholarship, and even ending up in the NFL. Understandably, the dads of the kids who make it beam with pride.

A few weeks before I quit my job at the Reagan Ranch, I wrote a long letter to my dad explaining why I was about to do what I was about to do. I put it all out there. It had all the dramatic language about how I had to do this or all that would be left of me was a shell of a man. I talked about following God's leading in my life and how I felt compelled to do this.

A few days passed and I had not heard back. Then a week passed. Finally, I called and asked if he'd gotten my letter. I said I was surprised I hadn't heard anything.

"What am I supposed to say?" was his reply. As far as he was concerned, I was making the biggest mistake of my life.

Over the next few years, as our life fell apart, I felt I could never be open with my parents and relay to them the struggles we were going through. After we settled in Lake Tahoe and began to get our footing again, I wrote to my dad and told him how much I'd been hurt by that experience. I hoped to bring the experience and the hurt out into the open so we could move on.

He apologized and I know that it truly hurt him to know that he had hurt me. Sadly, opening up to my dad brought little change to our relationship.

My dad's early career was similar to my own. He was young and successful and decided to go out on his own. His failure was about as dramatic as mine. My parents lost their house and our family ended up living in a barn on the outskirts of town that had been refurbished and made into apartments.

Maybe he was scared for me. Maybe that's why his reaction was so negative when I told him I was quitting my job. I've thought a lot about how I'd react someday if one of my kids told me they were doing something that I thought was a bad idea. I'd like to think I'd say something like:

"Oh, boy... Alright. Do you realize what you're getting into? Are you prepared to lose everything? Are you okay with that? Are you telling me you've got to do this? Go for it, man. Be prepared to have the shit kicked out of you... Have fun..."

Over time, as Monica and I went further down the path of life re-invention, the distance between us and my parents grew. I don't know if my parents don't understand or don't approve of our lifestyle. I don't know if I want to know. It'd hurt less if they had not been such good parents when I was growing up. I know people who have reached adulthood and they're just thankful to have made it and to be on their own because their childhood was so screwed up. That's not me. One of my favorite memories with my dad occurred when I was probably eight or nine years old. My parents had just put me to bed and I lay there trying to go to sleep in the midst of a thunderstorm. Suddenly, there was a dramatic flash of lightning and crack of thunder. I could feel the electricity go through my body and I screamed. I remember my dad rushing into the room. I was crying and he held me close while rocking, trying to console me.

When I was in middle school, my dad had a job where he drove a truck around Central Indiana filling vending machines. In the summer I went along with him everyday. I can't remember what he paid me to be his little assistant, but he didn't have to pay me. I would have gone for free. I sat on a seat of stacked soda cans with a few pillows for cushion and was happy as a clam.

That's what makes this so hard.

My parents helped mold me into the man that I am and I am grateful to them for all they've done for me. Through my middle school and high school years they encouraged me as a writer and during college, they did everything they could to support my pursuits, often giving me money they didn't really have to give.

Now, I feel like they barely know me, or even care to.

I can't dwell on it too much. My expectations with my parents have changed, and perhaps there will come a day when things will be different. I've had to move on and focus on what I do have.

What I do have is a wife with whom I am one. Together, we can pursue our dreams with reckless abandon. We both believe that even if things don't work out that we'll have a good story. We would both rather pursue our dreams and fail miserably than sit around and play it safe, disillusioned, burned out, or bored.

Teddy Roosevelt was right.

"It is not the critic who counts: not the man who points out how the strong man stumbles or where the doer of deeds could have done better. The credit belongs to the man who is actually in the arena, whose face is marred by dust and sweat and blood, who strives valiantly, who errs and comes up short again and again, because there is no effort without error or shortcoming, but who knows the great enthusiasms, the great devotions, who spends himself for a worthy cause; who, at the best, knows, in the end, the triumph of high achievement, and who, at the worst, if he fails, at least he fails while daring greatly, so that his place shall never be with those cold and timid souls who knew neither victory nor defeat."

Sadly, there will always be naysayers in this world. Sometimes they don't comprehend valuing passion over conventional wisdom.

Sometimes they feel jealous. Sometimes they fear having to pay social consequences for bucking the status quo.

There will also always be people who tell you that you're crazy and there will always be people who will tell you that you're awesome. The question, ultimately, isn't about what anyone else thinks.

Do you think you're crazy? (Keep in mind that a little bit of crazy is okay.)

Do you think you're awesome? (Keep in mind that a healthy self-esteem isn't a bad thing.)

Now, about that "mad" question.

Will you be more mad at yourself if you try, and fail, than if you never try at all?

That's a question only you can answer.

Act accordingly.

The Big Take-Aways

Take the time to figure out what you really want in life. Figure out what you are called to do or are wired to do, and then **resolve** to do it. If you have taken the time to do this, you must resolve that you will not allow yourself to be swayed by naysayers.

You must also **resolve** to be open and honest with friends about the direction you are going in life. Be transparent. Don't do what I did, which is put up a facade. The sooner you fully embrace the path you are on, the relationships that are built on trivial things will fade away. As you embrace your new life, new people who share your outlook will come into your life more quickly. Remember to not take it personally if people don't understand you or become angry with you.

Talk with your spouse or partner. Talk constantly. Make sure you're remaining on the same page and that you continue to have a shared vision. The best part is that when you determine to live the way you are wired to live, you become fully alive.

"The glory of God is a man fully alive." - St. Irenaeous

Action Steps

1. Do you have people in your life who would support you if you made the decision to re-invent your life. I'm not talking about having someone who'll let you live in their garage, although that sure is nice if it comes to that. My in-laws gave me something much more valuable than a roof over my family's head. They supported me in the process of re-inventing my life. If you're going to re-invent your life, there'll be lots of naysayers who say you're irresponsible or selfish or worse. You need people who will root for you and cheer you on. If you don't have those people in your life, find them. If you can't find anyone, contact me.

2. In addition to finding people who'll root for you, find people who are on the same path as you. Find people who share your vision for the future and are trying to achieve something similar with their own lives. It's great if you can find this in your own community, but

if you can't, look for it online. Some of my closest friends are people I've never met in person. They are friends I've met online who share similar goals who I interact with regularly. If you don't know where to look, contact me and let me help you.

"Don't begin until you count the cost. For who would begin construction of a building without first calculating the cost."

Luke 14:28

CHAPTER 6

It ain't always easy

A while back, an online friend who I've never met in person but who shares similar goals in terms of lifestyle design sent me a private message on Facebook. She said I hadn't seemed like my cheery self lately and wanted to check in to make sure everything was okay. Her message sent me into a self-led 48-hour psychoanalysis. I had not noticed that I was not my "cheery self" lately, but her message prompted some self-reflection. *Was I unhappy?*

The previous few months had certainly had their share of difficulties. At the same time, I didn't feel unhappy. Was I subconsciously unhappy? Had my friend identified in me something I had not yet seen in myself?

◆

HAVE KIDS, WILL TRAVEL

To put this all in context, at that time our family had just re-turned to the States after six weeks of travel in Central America. On both the front-end and back-end of our time in Central America, we spent time in the in-laws garage in Santa Barbara. The total duration of our trip, from the time we left our home in Lake Tahoe to the time we returned, was two months.

We returned to Tahoe with ski season already in full swing and it was time to hit the slopes. We were also returning to Tahoe the first week of December and I love Christmas. We were decking our halls and celebrating the season.

We lead an unbelievable life.

The previous summer, before our travels in Central America, was one of those summers we'll never forget. The kids were riding bikes for the first time and we spent so much time at the beach together. When we left for Central America, Monica was four months preg-nant with our daughter Abigail. Now back in Lake Tahoe, we were preparing to welcome a new baby into our family.

It's ridiculous. It's such an awesome life that it's ridiculous.

I made a commitment, though, that on our blog and on social media that I would tell the whole story. If all I ever talked about were the great parts of our life, you may jump into the abyss like we have before you count the costs. Blogs and social media can some-times turn into highlight reels and a game of one-upmanship, so I'm committed to talking about the awesome stuff we get to do and the utterly chaotic situations we sometimes put ourselves in.

Even though we've come a long way financially, we knew that our Central America trip was going to be a stretch for us. We were taking a six week trip through foreign countries when a few years earlier we were living with the in-laws. That's an accomplishment. That's progress. We were doing something that two years earlier we could have only dreamed of. Still, the trip was a stretch.

Our Central America travels were loaded with happy and seren-dipitous moments. On our son's fifth birthday, we went to the top of a volcano and roasted marshmallows on cooling lava. In Honduras we toured Mayan ruins and held magnificent macaws on our arms. From the island of Utilia we hopped a ride with a fisherman and had a tiny little island to ourselves for a day and swam in the crystal clear waters of the Caribbean. In El Salvador, we played on black sand beaches. We interacted with locals and fellow travelers. We connect-ed with other traveling families we'd met online. We breathed deeply and lived fully. It was an incredible six weeks.

There's another side to the story though. Monica and I both continue working wherever we are. Back home in the States, people would refer to our six weeks in Central America as a vacation. It was not a vacation; it was just life. We had our laptops and kept working much like we would work at home. While we were in Central Amer-ica, some projects stalled. Some money we were planning on coming in did not come in and things started to get tight. We budgeted tightly, spending all but our few last dollars by the time we arrived at the San Pedro Sula International Airport to fly back to California.

Things were about to get very stressful.

In a moment of desperation I turned to the crowd behind me — about two dozen travelers standing in line waiting to pay their exit fees to leave Honduras — and I pulled my phone out of my pocket and held it in the air.

"Does anyone want to buy my iPhone?"

Eyes of confusion gazed on my family and me.

In order to board our flight home to the United States, we each — me, my wife, and our two kids — had to pay a $38 exit fee. $38 X 4 = $152. All the money we had left was $11US and some Limperas, the Honduran currency. We were more than plenty short and there was no getting on that plane until we each paid our taxes.

They say the only things certain in life are death and taxes and I can tell you, in that moment, the taxes were absolutely certain. We talked to official after official; waited in one line and then another. The clock was ticking and soon our flight would be departing. The kids began to sense something was wrong and on a very short night of sleep, tears started to appear in their eyes.

"I want to see grandma...."

We called grandma — my wife's parents in California — where it was 4:00 o'clock in the morning. Her parents have a debit card tied to our checking account for moments just like this one. They rushed to the bank and deposited a check into the ATM. We waited a few moments and had the officials run our card.

Declined.

I checked our account online and there was a glitch in the bank's system. The check was not showing up. We'd exhorted to our last resort and our last resort had not worked. Our flight was already boarding and would soon be departing. That's when I turned to the crowd behind us.

"Does anyone want to buy my iPhone?"

I looked into a crowd of blank stares.

"We have no money," I explained, "and we cannot get on our flight to go home until we pay our exit fees."

What happened next totally overwhelmed us. People began pulling out their pocket books and asking how much money we needed. A woman walked up and handed us money. A man grabbed my arm and I turned to look at him and he handed me a $100 bill. My eyes were welling up with tears; tears of gratitude streamed down Monica's face.

I handed all of the money to the officials who began working on our passports. I began trying to find each person who'd helped us and thank them. Then, just like that, we were gone. We rushed up the stairs, through security, and onto our flight. We'd be rescued by total strangers we'll never see again.

How had we let ourselves get in that situation? What kind of person travels into foreign countries with so little financial margin? Are we irresponsible? Bad parents? I wrestled with all of those questions on our flight home.

Back in California, it was time to get to work. We needed to make some money and just when we did, we got hit with a major car repair bill. We got back home to Tahoe, and after two months away we had the expense of re-stocking our house.

Even though we had experienced and were experiencing amazing things, it had been a hard couple of months financially and on social media I hadn't pulled the veil over these difficulties. Hence the message from my friend on Facebook.

Here's what I'm getting at: our life isn't perfect. If I only tell you about the cool things we're seeing in Antigua or about the great day I had skiing, I'm not telling you the whole story. I'm not complaining about the struggles. We're happy with the choices we've made. But you need the full picture.

◆

WORK IN PROGRESS

Our society is designed for people to live a certain way. There's a reason why the vast majority of people do the same thing. There's a reason why there are so many people who are W-2 employees in the United States. Our societal structure accommodates one type of lifestyle and there are going to be challenges associated with living differently.

As we have built a life of our own design, we've often been like a duck on water. We look graceful to someone casually watching, but below the surface there's a lot going on. As we began to build our patchwork of income, we had some steady income, but not enough to fully sustain us. We depended on other work, which wasn't guaranteed and often sporadic. Then, as anyone who is self-employed can attest, actually getting paid for the work you did can be a challenge. As a result, sometimes things were very tight. Finding things around our house to sell on Craiglist in order to get gas money has not been uncommon in our house. And then one day we end up in San Pedro Sula without enough money to pay exit fees.

Of course, I'd like it to be easier. It's gotten easier since that 2012 Central America trip. We traveled for three months in Thailand with plenty of financial margin and I've got to tell you that felt very liberating. When we had to admit our one-year-old daughter to the hospital in Chiang Mai we weren't worried about money. It took a while for us to learn how to really make enough money on our terms and when we were in Central America we hadn't really figured it out all that well yet. A few years later, we're better at it and in a few years I expect to be better still. I quit my job in 2008, but we didn't get on this "alternative" lifestyle design until a few years later. There've been times I've felt like we're close to getting everything figured out, but then I realize we're still a long way off. Not only is there a learning curve, it also takes time to build momentum.

I just want to give you a real picture of what our life looks like.

You have to consider what you're willing to accept in terms of struggle in order to achieve a life of your own design. This life isn't for you if you're lazy. It takes hard work. You've got to want it – and I mean *really* want it.

Piecing this all together and achieving the kind of freedom we aspire is not easy. It's hard. It would be easier to just go get a job, but I can't just get a job. That's not the way I'm wired.

When I quit my job, I said to my wife that if things did not work out financially, I could always go back to the grind. This life we live is like crack, though. Once you get a taste you can't stop; you just figure out a way to keep it going.

The Big Take-Aways

It ain't always easy! Don't jump off into the abyss and think that everything is going to work out perfectly. Great stories don't develop that way and you want your story to be great! Before I quit my job at the Reagan Ranch, I had to mentally prepare myself for the possibility of failure. A friend asked me, "Clark, if I told you that the deal with the cafe was not going to go through, would you still quit?" My answer was yes because I knew I was following my heart and following God's leading in my life. Hold everything loosely. Determine what you want -- your dream -- and put everything else on the chopping block. Have things but possess nothing, which is to say, it's okay to have things but don't let things have you.

I feel very strongly that I need to communicate how precarious our situation has been at times because I don't want to paint too rosy a picture, have you throw caution to the wind... and then blame me for not telling you how hard this is! It's hard, but it's totally worth it!

Action Steps

1. How do you react to stress? Do you retreat? Innovate? Blame others? How would you like to react to stress?

2. You've heard the saying, "The grass is always greener on the other side of the fence." People's lives aren't always easy. Most people won't tell you the whole story. Our life isn't always easy, but let me ask you this: "Is your life always easy now? Do you deal with financial stress? If the answer to these questions is yes, then what do you have to lose?

3. Make a list of non-negotiable items. Think about this as a safety blanket. What are you not willing to do without? Then start letting go of everything else.

"I went to the woods because I wished to live deliberately...and not, when I came to die, discover that I had not lived... I wanted to live deep and suck out all the marrow of life, to live so sturdily and Spartan-like as to put to rout all that was not life, to cut a broad swath and shave close, to drive life into a corner, and reduce it to its lowest terms."

Henry David Thoreau

CHAPTER 7

Let's Make a Deal

After I lost my election for United States Congress, our family went on a trip to Seattle. We traveled up the coast by train and spent a week in the Emerald City. It was really an amazing time. Over the previous few months, we'd spent so little time together as a family. Although we had a full-time staffer on my campaign, Monica ran the operation and the kids were with us on the campaign trail more often than not. While there had been plenty of time together, it wasn't the rich, quality time you long for with your most important relationships. The last several weeks of the campaign, Monica and I had lots of Jack in the Box dinners at one o'clock in the morning.

When we boarded the train to Seattle we had enough money to get there, have fun and get home. That was it. After that, we'd have to figure something else out.

Some people might consider it irresponsible to take all the money you have to your name and blow it on a trip. (By now, you've probably figured out that I think differently...). I figure, unless I make more money, running out of it is inevitable. I could spend the money I had in Santa Barbara or I could spend it in Seattle. What's the difference? We'd go to Seattle, spend some time together as a family, and wait for the next opportunity to present itself.

When we got home the waiting continued. Our home was empty. The cupboards were empty. The refrigerator was empty. The emptiness went deeper, though. We didn't feel at home anymore. Every evening we'd go over to the in-laws house for dinner. We'd stay until it was bedtime for the kids, then come home and put them to bed. Monica and I would then stay up talking about what we were going to do.

I don't remember feeling depressed when we finally made the decision to move into the in-laws garage. I remember feeling relieved. Our life in that house those last few months was miserable. I didn't care where we were moving, I was just happy to be moving.

◆

THE BIG SWAP

The great gift that my in-laws gave me was not a roof over my head. They gave me the gift of time. Without them, I would have been forced to grasp for any job I could get my hands on. The job I almost took -- the one I realized I didn't believe in -- without my in-laws I have to take that job and I am forced to give away my life in the name of survival. Because I had the gift of time, I became a credit card processing rep and began building up a passive, residual income stream.

In the beginning, we were making so little money. Having our income grow so slowly turned out to be an amazing thing for us.

When we were living in the in-laws garage and then later in Monica's grandfather's cabin in Tahoe, we were a bare-bones operation. We had to think about every little expense. The first winter we lived in Tahoe I often went to a men's Bible study at my church. There was a dinner each week before the study began and everyone was asked to chip in $5 to help cover the cost of the meal. I remember that being a big deal. We had to plan for that weekly $5 expense.

Whenever we spent money -- especially if we were adding something that was going to be an ongoing expense -- it was only after a lot of thought and a lot of discussion.

It's not like we made nothing and had nothing and then one day I took a job making a $50,000 annual salary. Go from nothing to $50,000 that quickly and you start spending money quickly. You're getting cable internet and then decide to add cable television and cable phone services, because you know, it's a better deal if you bundle your services. Then come the gym memberships and fat cell phone plans. You finance a new car and your insurance premiums go up.

Pretty soon, you're as broke as the guy living in his in-laws garage. You've got a lot of stuff, but you're broke.

The experience of going down to nothing and then slowly and methodically building our income up again forever changed our relationship with money.

All the stuff we have in life -- house, cars, toys -- we have because we've made a trade. We trade a part of our life to get money and then we trade that money to get stuff. More directly, whatever we have in life in terms of material possessions, we have because we've traded a part of our life to get it.

Think about that for a second.

How much of my life am I willing to trade for a million dollar house in Santa Barbara?

How much of my life am I willing to trade for unlimited data on my smart phone plan?

How much of my life am I willing to trade for cable television in my house?

How much of my life am I willing to trade for flights to Thailand?

These are questions that I've got to ask myself. There are not necessarily any right or wrong answers. It's about being honest with myself and understanding the direct correlation between my time, my money, and my possessions. If I'm going to trade a part of my life for something, I'd better make darn sure that I want it. *I want to make a good trade.*

◆

TWO BIRDS, ONE STONE

When we were more permanently settled in Tahoe, during our long winters, we heated our home primarily with a wood-burning stove. We went through a lot of wood.

The process began each spring after the snow melted. I would go out into the forest and gather large rounds of wood that are left as a part of fire prevention being done by the forest service. Then, I had to split those rounds, which I did partly by hand with my 30 pound maul and I would also rent a splitter for a day or two. Once all that wood was split, then it had to be stacked.

It was a big job and it would generally take me from late May to early October to complete the work. I loved it because I felt like I was being super efficient with my life energy.

By heating our home with a wood-burning stove, we saved a lot of money in the winter on our electric bill, plus sitting by the fire at night with my wife is much more romantic than sitting by the furnace!

Although I did trade a lot of my life in this process, I felt like I got a lot out of it. It's a big workout. There's a lot of sweat and a lot of energy expended. With all this hard physical work, I had no need for a gym membership. Not only would I have to pay for a gym membership (which is to say trade a part of my life for a gym membership), but the energy I expend at a gym on a treadmill is spent and then gone. The energy I spend gathering, splitting and stacking wood is actually used for something. I would think about this all summer long, through every step of the firewood process. I got a tremendous amount of satisfaction knowing that my sweat was going right into that stove and it would keep us warm all winter.

It also cleared my head. When I was working on the wood, I would think. I'd be sorting through issues in my mind. This project wasn't just about physical well-being, it also contributed to my mental well-being. I didn't have to add the cost of seeing a shrink to my monthly budget!

For me, this was a great trade. I felt really good about the exchange. I traded a part of my life and in return I got physical exercise, mental health and I heated my home.

Because we've moved out of a long-term lease in Tahoe and now only return to vacation rentals during the winter, this annual process is on hold. Eventually, we'll likely return to a long-term housing situation in Lake Tahoe. Our plan is to eventually buy a home in Tahoe and when we do, the wood will again be a part of my life and I'll gather, split and stack my way to physical and mental health while heating our home.

You may think I'm crazy. This may sound like a terrible trade to you. You may happily sit down at your computer and go to work to make enough money to run the furnace all winter or just have a great big pile of wood delivered to your doorstep.

But are you asking the question?

What are you trading your life for?

Are you making a good trade?

I'm not asking you to be cheap. I'm asking you to think.

What I'm trying to do is make sure that where I spend my money -- which is to say, where I spend my life energy -- lines up with what I value most.

My friend Bryan, the self-employed entrepreneur who I referred to earlier, thinks that many of my expenses are frivolous. Monica and I love going to swanky bars and drinking expensive martinis. To him, those martinis are over-priced, because he does not place a high value on that experience. To me, the martinis are priced just right because I place a high value on that experience.

I think a lot of people look at our life and think that we must be millionaires. Afterall, we do live like millionaires! How else could we afford to travel so much? How else could we afford to do all the skiing we do? How else could we afford those swanky bars and expensive martinis?

We must be rich, right?

What people falsely assume is that we have all the things they have, and we travel too. No, we don't have all those things. We've given up lots of stuff that modern American culture thinks are essential. There are lots of no's in our life.

Shortly after Monica and I were married, the band U2 was on tour and they were coming through California. I'm a huge U2 fan and we were buying tickets to several of their shows. A co-worker enviously said that I must be getting paid really well in order to be able to afford all those tickets. It wasn't that I was being paid really well, it was that I knew what I really wanted. I wanted to see U2. It was a priority. I was going to make it happen.

We have whatever we really want in life. If you really want to travel or you want to ski or you want to go see U2, give up other things that matter less.

I'd love to have cable or satellite television service in our house. I'd love to be able to come home on a Sunday and be around the house with football on all day. I'd love that. But I don't love it as much as I love to travel. Maybe I can't travel very far on the money I save by not having cable television, but lots of little decisions add up.

You can understand what I value in life just by observing me. This is true of everyone. Our lives are a true reflection of what we value most. That's why I spend so much time thinking about this, because I want my life to be a true reflection of the deepest places of my heart. I want to spend my life energy wisely.

If you had something of infinite value, how carefully would you think before parting with it? Think hard about this question because you do have something of infinite value. It's your life.

What are you trading your life for?

The Big Take-Aways

Time is an irreplaceable resource. You are running out of time. You have less time now than when you began reading this book. (I hope you think you are making a good trade). Think about what you want in life. Don't look at yourself through the filter of other people's lives. Don't react. Don't merely respond to stimuli. This is what marketers want you to do. Corporations and marketers have become very adept at reaching potential customers at their weakest moments. You have to think about what you want in life and be deliberate about it, so when you do spend money (your life energy) you know you are spending wisely.

Action Steps

1. How are you wasting your life right now? What are some bad trades you are making?

2. How can you make better trades? What are some things you don't really want to give up but you could get at a better value?

3. How can you combine ways you expend life energy and "kill two birds with one stone." When I am working on my wood pile, I am exercising and heating my home. When I am skiing, I am getting exercise and enjoying one of my favorite recreational activities.

4. What are some of the really good trades you are making? Why are these good trades? What are the underlying values that make these good trades?

"Money often costs too much."

Ralph Waldo Emerson

CHAPTER 8

Patchwork Income

I want to spend my life energy wisely. I don't know when my time will expire. Chances are, I have many more years on this earth. Am I really reinventing my life only because I have this awareness there's a slim chance I could soon die?

There are other great (and less morbid) reasons that Monica and I have designed our life this way. Our kids are one reason. Why work my butt off now, while my kids are at home, so I can relax when they are gone? Why wait until I am old to travel the world? Why wait until I am 60 to ski 60 days a year?

I once participated in an interview and when the interview was published the teaser made note of the fact that I ski 60 days a year, spend almost as many days at the beach in the summer and had just wrapped up a six-week trip to Central America with my family.

"Naturally," the teaser continued, "this type of freedom is best accomplished without a job."

What?

I often get job offers that would pay me really good money, but the money I would make isn't as valuable as what I have now. Don't get me wrong: I like money and the things that money can buy. I'd like to have more money and more of the things that money can buy. *But only on my terms.*

Most people approach life and say: *I want to get the highest-paying job possible and then take the money and buy the best life possible.*

What I'm suggesting is that we say: *I want to have the best life possible. How do I get the money I need to fund it?*

How do I ski 60 days a year, spend just as many at the beach in the summer and have the freedom to travel. How is it that without a "job" I have the financial ability to spend three months with my family in Thailand? How can we afford to bounce around the United States for six months or longer? How is it possible that I'm able to spend pretty much all day every day with my family? How is it possible that if I decide tomorrow I want to leave town and not come back for a month, I could?

The answer? Patchwork income.

What is patchwork income? Picture a quilt with several patches in varying sizes. Patchwork income is the concept of funding your life through several patches of income. Some patches are larger than others but all of the patches, no matter how small, are necessary.

The patches look different and each have their own character. For Monica and me, our friends look at the varying types of patches and are often amazed by their variety. When people ask us "what do you do?" we don't know what to say. Some projects we work on could pay us multiple thousands of dollars and some projects may pay us only a few dollars. It's all a part of our patchwork.

With money coming from several sources, while our bank account sometimes has a low balance, we are almost never out of money. We do sometimes run out of money (like at the airport in San Pedro Sula) but when that happens there are usually several potential payments that could come our way within days or, in some cases, even hours. One client may be slow to pay and that's frustrating, but it's unlikely that all of our sources of income will be stalled at any one time.

Without realizing what we were doing, we began building our patchwork when Monica started finding $5 gigs online while living in the in-laws garage. Then we added in money I made as a credit card processing rep. Then I landed a consulting gig. And we'd started our patchwork. We're better patchworkers now than we were when we started. Experience and momentum should both make us better still in time.

When it comes to investing, experts say that it is good to diversify. Don't have all your money in real estate. Have some real estate. Have some stocks. Have some bonds. Diversity is something that experts swear by when it comes to retirement savings. If diversity is such a good idea for retirement savings, why not apply the same principle to income?

In the post Great Recession world, the idea of having a "secure job" is an illusion. When I quit my job, there were people who thought I was crazy for giving up my "secure job." But my employer, or the economy, could have taken that job from me at any moment and that job was my only source of income. How is that security? Being completely dependent on a "job" for your income is like having all your eggs in one basket.

Because we have a patchwork of income instead of one source of income, if something happens and we lose any one sources of income, the effect would not be catastrophic. It would hurt if something happened to one of the larger patches, but still, the effect would not be devastating. We would not be destitute and we could survive on other income, go to work on other pieces of our patchwork and slowly (hopefully not too slowly) replace that missing patch.

When Monica was an employee making a set salary, she felt limited. I had really never known or thought differently; for the majority of my life, my parents were typical W-2 employees. Monica's parents had owned their own businesses. Monica also started a surf board business with her parents when she graduated from college. In those settings, she always had the hope of making more money. You could come up with an idea or make a deal. Unexpected car repair bill? Time to find a new client. As an employee that's not the case. As an employee, you're simply cashing a check every two weeks.

With our patchwork income approach, we can always make more money. Our income isn't set. As patchwork incomers, we don't "ask" for a raise. We get it by either getting more work or figuring out how to create something of greater value. The last time I ever asked for a raise was 2006, as I entered into my final year of being an employee. I don't ever plan to ask someone for a raise again in my life. I haven't asked for a day off in years.

Patchwork income differs somewhat from "freelance work" or "consulting" in that people who describe themselves as freelancers or consultants are typically freelancing or consulting in a particular field. For example, you have freelance writers or political consultants.

A patchwork incomer may work in many fields. As a patchwork incomer, I'm both a freelancer and a consultant. I'm a freelance writer and blogger. I'm a fundraising consultant for nonprofit organizations. I'm an independent contractor as a credit card processing rep. I work in marketing and promotion. I'm a life coach. Monica works with me on each of these and and also builds websites and smartphone apps and is a business consultant. Together, Monica and I launched TahoeSkiBum.com.

One of the greatest benefits of patchwork income is the freedom to explore. Our life is full of side projects. TahoeSkiBum.com, which we believe will believe will come to be a significant piece of our patchwork, was started as a side project. We've poured hundreds of hours and significant resources into building the site and community that surrounds it. We have the ability to invest hundreds of hours into a project without pay because of the diversity of our income. Monica's smartphone apps came out of a side project. We'll do anything that provides the right combination of money (or potential money) and intrigue. I can't tell you how many things we've tried that have not worked. That's the adventurous part of patchwork income: if there's something you want to do that you think you can make money at, go for it. Patchwork income has given me the freedom to explore new things I never would have considered as an employee or even as a freelancer or consultant.

By keeping our expenses low -- one of our three financial tenants I discussed earlier -- the power of patchwork income is further leveraged. What may be considered a small piece of a patchwork to some is a much larger piece to us because we've committed to keeping our expenses low.

We have also discovered the currency of barter as a part of our patchwork. Remember, I don't care how much money I make, I care about my quality of life. So if I do some work for a restaurant in exchange for credit, that's great. It's easier for the restaurant to give me $100 a month in credit than it is for them to write me a check. We are paid in barter and we also pay in barter.

I'm not interested in making a particular amount of money. What I'm after is a particular kind of life. If I can do work with and for people and trade that part of my life energy for things that I want or need, I have added another piece to my patchwork and increased my wealth.

Arriving at this point was a long process for us. This is not what I quit my job to do when I left the Reagan Ranch in 2008. I quit to buy a cafe. When that did not work out, I transitioned to building a consultancy. After my campaign for Congress when I became a credit card processing rep and Monica was getting gigs online, we were beginning to build a patchwork, but it was not a philosophy or concept that we thought about.

I can't tell you exactly when we did become patchwork incomers. Slowly, the term worked its way into our family vocabulary. Slowly, we began to realize and enjoy the benefits of patchwork income. Slowly, we began to embrace patchwork income as our overarching financial strategy to achieve a life of our own design.

In 2008 this was not our plan. Steve Jobs once said, "You can't connect the dots looking forward you can only connect them looking backwards. So you have to trust that the dots will somehow connect in your future. You have to trust in something: your gut, destiny, life, karma, whatever. Because believing that the dots will connect down the road will give you the confidence to follow your heart, even when it leads you off the well worn path."

Looking back, we can see how our successes and our failures all brought us to where we are today. We've invested lots of time in things that have not worked out. That's okay. All that we have experienced has helped us build our patchwork of income and live a life of our own design.

Once we realized what we were doing -- how we had accidentally started building this amazing patchwork -- I determined that I would never depend on a single source of income for our family. We would make a beautiful patchwork.

When we began creating our patchwork, we were really struggling financially. We had to focus on income. I needed to close accounts. I needed to book consulting gigs. Over time, we regained our financial footing and the patchwork provided us the security to begin the process of figuring out what we *loved*.

We had the lifestyle we wanted. For me, part of living epicly is engaging in work that I'm passionate about. I wanted to do great work and I believed the only way to do great work was to do work that I loved.

That was the patch I was searching for.

The Big Take-Aways

Most people approach life with the goal of finding the *highest-paying job possible* and then take that money they make at that job and buy the best life possible. My assertion is that we should figure out how to have the *have the best life possible*. Once you know how you can have the best life possible, the next question is figuring out how to make enough money to have that kind of life.

Patchwork income brings the idea of "diversification" to income. If diversification is such a good idea for retirement savings, why not bring the idea to income? Patchwork income is making money in lots of different ways from lots of different sources. By having a diversified portfolio of income streams, you have greater security. If you have a job, you only have one source of income. That means if you lose your job, you lose all of your income. With patchwork income, it's virtually impossible (or at least highly, highly unlikely) that you could lose all of your income.

Patchwork income works best when you keep your expenses low because little bits of money that you make here and there have a greater impact on your overall budget. The idea of Patchwork Income also allows you to try new things that could become new passions in your life.

Action Steps

1. Make a list of three projects you could potentially work on. Maybe you'd like to quit your jobs to do something different, but you can't think of any one thing you could do to make enough money to sustain life as you envision it. Think of three projects you could work on to begin "piecing it together." This is the beginning of your patchwork.

2. What skills have you gained in your current career and in your life experiences? Make a list.

3. What do you love? What are your hobbies? How could you make money doing these things?

"All courses of action are risky, so prudence is not in avoiding danger (it's impossible), but in calculating risk and acting decisively. Make mistakes of ambition and not mistakes of sloth. Develop the strength to do bold things, not the strength to suffer."

-Machiavelli

CHAPTER 9

Choose Your Risk

I can't imagine what it must have been like to be a member of the graduating class of Stanford University in 2005. If you're wondering what was so special about that particular graduating class and that particular day, there's a good chance that all you need to do is pull your phone out of your pocket for a clue. If it's an iPhone, you're on the right track.

On June 12, 2005, Steve Jobs gave the commencement address to the crowd of newly minted Stanford alums. As I have gone through the process of re-inventing my life, I have watched that speech on countless occasions and have read the text dozens more. In the address, Steve Jobs talks about the experience of being fired from Apple when he was 30 years old, the same age I was when I lost my campaign for Congress and moved my family into the in-laws garage.

What he says rings true for me.

"So at 30 I was out. And very publicly out. What had been the focus of my entire adult life was gone and it was devastating."

When I lost my bid for Congress, I was out. Maybe not as publicly out as Steve Jobs when he was fired from Apple, but certainly, what had been the focus of my entire adult life was gone. I found myself at a loss and sensed that I was at a turning point in my life.

Steve Jobs, at that moment, contemplated walking away. He considered leaving Silicon Valley and starting over somewhere else, pursuing a different life. You could say he considered the possibility that he would re-invent his life.

"But something slowly began to dawn on me," Jobs continues. "I still loved what I did...I had been rejected, but I was still in love. And so I decided to start over." Steve Jobs dusted himself off and got back in the game. He got back in the game because he realized he still loved it.

When I lost my campaign for Congress, I was three times a loser. I had failed at my attempt to acquire and develop the cafe, failed at my attempt to grow a consulting agency and failed in my bid for Congress.

I could have dusted myself off and gotten back in the game. My heart wasn't in it though, so I stopped. Many people mistake activity for progress, but I needed to reassess my life and this is when I took a step further into the void. In 2008 I quit my job but not to re-invent my life. In 2008 I made the decision to quit my job at the Reagan Ranch, but my life post-Reagan Ranch was not radically different. Quitting may have been a bold decision, but remember, quitting was not a decision to "leave the game." I was just going to play the game in a different way. After my campaign, I quit playing the game. I was 30 years old. Losing a campaign for Congress shouldn't be devastating, but I was like an athlete walking away in the middle of a successful career because their heart's not in it. My heart wasn't in it anymore, so I walked away. I didn't give up on my political aspirations because I lacked the tenacity. I felt beat up, but had I been in love with it, I could have dusted myself off a hundred more times.

I wanted to do work that I loved. I had once loved my work at the Reagan Ranch. In a 31 page memo -- my version of a Jerry McGuire mission statement -- that I had bound and distributed to our staff in 2007, I wrote:

"We are blessed to have the jobs we have... How can we not be totally engaged in this? It should consume us. Some people will spend their entire lives trying to prevent themselves from being defined by their jobs. We should embrace this. Let our jobs define us. How else would we want to be defined?"

I wanted to be engaged in something that made me feel that way again.

My in-laws gave me the gift of time by putting a roof over my family's head. Their generosity allowed me to slowly and methodically build up a base of income from my portfolio of credit card processing accounts. With an income base in place, I then gave myself the gift of time. With income automatically coming in every month, I was able to try lots of things in search of work that I loved.

Our world needs more people doing what they love.

Our world, collectively, is poorer than it should be because people have settled for work they don't love. When you love your work, you produce great work. The more people there are in this world producing great work, the richer we all become.

"If you haven't found it yet, keep looking. Don't settle." (Jobs)

Maybe this all sounds a little crazy to you. Maybe it's pie in the sky. Maybe it smacks of arrogance and ungratefulness. Steve Jobs made his comments way back in 2005, before the Great Recession. Shouldn't loving your work just be the icing on the cake? Maybe you're thinking it's great if you can find a job you love, but you shouldn't expect it. Just be thankful for what you do have, whether you love it or not. "The economy being what it is," you say, "long-term benefits running out..."

There's so much uncertainty out there. Yes, I'll grant you that. There is uncertainty. And there's risk. That's all there is, though. There are no guarantees. There is no security. There's no job that can give you those things. The only choice that you have is choosing between risk that is unsatisfying or risk that is satisfying.

Figure out what you love so you can take the risk that is satisfying. You can try to mitigate risk. Our patchwork income approach is a strategy to mitigate risk. Yet still, the best laid plans of mice and men are but the plans of mice and men.

I'm thankful for the work I have that I do not love. That work has provided substantial income for our family, but I won't stop there. I want to give the world the best of me. I believe there's something beautiful in all of us that we have to give the world. I want to give that thing that is in me to the world.

If I had stopped at saying, "I'm a credit card processing rep," that would have also meant I was stopping searching for the patch I loved. Our patchwork paid the bills and allowed us to live life on our terms while also giving us the space to keep trying new things, each thing bringing us closer to what we love.

"As with all matters of the heart, you'll know when you find it." (Jobs)

One thing I re-discovered is that I love writing. Writing is a passion I first discovered in middle school but somewhere along the way discarded. By writing this book, I am doing something that I love. I hope that by writing this I have made the world just a tiny bit richer.

As our patchwork began to grow, I made the decision to get out of consulting to non-profits. I only kept the clients that I enjoyed working with the most and fit a very particular niche. What I discovered is that I loved this type of work, and that I was really good at it. Because we had financial latitude, I could make the decision to get out of consulting. Over time, I learned that I didn't want to get out of consulting, I just needed to stop taking on the wrong type of clients. I was on my way to eliminating this patch, but instead it has grown. Without the patchwork income philosophy, this process does not happen.

While seeking work that I truly love, I've discovered other things I would have never dreamed of doing just a few years ago. I love managing our website TahoeSkiBum.com. Years ago I could have never imagined I would be doing this. I can spend endless hours working on Tahoe Ski Bum and it does not feel like work. It is a passion. l love it. I hope that in some small way by creating this site Monica and I have made the world a tiny bit richer.

Remember, you can't connect the dots looking forward. Steve Jobs could have never predicted how important a calligraphy class he crashed as a college dropout would later be to developing the typography for the first Mac computer. I could have never imagined when I went on my first ski trip in 2008 that I would now own a website about skiing and snowboarding in Lake Tahoe. When we're pursuing the things that we love instead of just dollars, the universe has a way of conspiring to help us get the dollars we need from the things we love.

Consider the "safe path" where you just get a job and stop complaining. You collect a steady paycheck, and when the day almost certainly comes when you lose that job for whatever reason, it'll be hard for a while, but surely, relatively soon, you'll have a new job. You'll again collect a steady paycheck. If you are lucky, you'll have enough left over to begin saving for retirement. You'll probably, eventually be downsized from that job and you'll end up burning through a chunk of that retirement savings. But keep on this track long enough and you'll probably, eventually be able to retire.

Sigh.

I'm trying to live a life I never want to retire from. Don't you want that kind of life too? I want to be engaged in work that I never want to quit because I love it. And if the love fades, I want to find new work that I can engage in that makes me feel alive all over again.

In the movie *Up in the Air*, the character Ryan Bingham, played by George Clooney, is letting Bob in on the unfortunate news that he's being downsized. Bob's none too happy.

Ryan Bingham: *I'm not a shrink, Bob, I'm a wake up call. You know why kids love athletes?*

Bob: *I don't know, because they screw lingerie models...*

Ryan Bingham: *No, that's why we love athletes. Kids love athletes because they followed their dreams.*

Bob: *Well I can't dunk.*

Ryan Bingham: *No, but you can cook.*

Bob: *What are you talking about?*

Ryan Bingham: *Your resume says you minored in French Culinary Arts. Most students work the frier at KFC. You bused tables at Il Picatorre to support yourself. Then you got out of college and started working here. How much did they pay you to give up on your dreams?*

Bob: *Twenty seven grand a year.*

Ryan Bingham: *At what point were you going to stop and go back to what made you happy?*

Life is uncertain. Choose your risk. Will you choose risk that is unsatisfying or risk that satisfies?

Choose work you love. Choose epic work, not just because you love it, but because you have something to offer the world that nobody else does. I beg you to share it.

The world is waiting.

The Big Take-Aways

Don't fall into the trap of thinking you are being selfish by pursuing work that you love. Pursuing work that you love will make you come alive, but just as importantly, there's a gift in you that you have the opportunity to give to the world. Don't hold back. Give it.

And while it may sound scary to "go for it," it's no more risky than staying in a job you don't love. There is no security in the job market today. There's no such thing anymore as a safe or secure job. Your choice is not between playing it safe and taking a risk. Your choice is between risk that is unsatisfying or risk that satisfies.

Action Steps

1. Do you love your work? Are you engaged in work that you are passionate about? Do you believe the world is getting the best of you? I don't ask these questions flippantly so please don't answer them flippantly.

2. If you were laid off from your job tomorrow and because of some strange twist in the cosmos, you were completely restricted and unable to continue in your current career path or field, what type of work would you want to do?

3. Was there some class or extracurricular activity you participated in when you were in high school or college that made you come alive that you have not thought about in a long time? Have you buried a dream?

"*Love does not consist in gazing at each other, but in looking outward together in the same direction.*"

Antoine de Saint-Exupery

CHAPTER 10

Σat, Talk, Make Love

As Abraham Lincoln famously said, *"A house divided against itself cannot stand."* If you are married or in a committed relationship, accomplishing your goals in life will be almost impossible if you and your partner are not of one heart and one mind. Because of that, this chapter may be the most important chapter of this book.

My wife has been married to three men and yet she has never been divorced.

She married a young go-getter. A young man who was in a hurry to get things done and get ahead. He loved his job, he was successful, he made a lot of money and he spent even more money.

She then married a hip, young entrepreneur. Her first husband wore business suits. Her new husband wore designer jeans and trendy shirts. He had big, audacious dreams. He was ready to put it all on the line and he did.

She then married a family man with a propensity to be a ski bum. Her third husband is home most days with the kids. By summer, board shorts and t-shirts are his attire. He has a few suits in the closet that he can pull out for a business trip. His work is pieced together. He has clients to serve but he's not really tied down. He loves to travel, but not necessarily on business. He loves family travel.

I am of course all three men.

Occasionally people say something to me like, *"Your wife must really love you with the roller coaster you've put her on."*

Monica is as crazy as I am. Monica is the one who graduated from college with a degree in architecture... and used that experience as a segue into launching a surfboard company. She and her dad flew up to Kirkland, Washington to pitch Costco on selling their boards. Costco bought it, and at the end of the meeting asked, "When can you start?" Monica's dad said, "Two weeks."

They had zero surfboards.

So they went to work to be ready for their opening day with Costco. I met Monica just as the surfboard company was about to go belly-up. I remember going on a walk with her and there was a sense of disappointment, but mainly, there was a sense of "who cares." You roll the dice, you play the game. She then parlayed her experience in the surfboard industry to move to Ireland for a year to work with a local church. After she returned to the States she went to work for a prestigious architectural firm and later went out on her own. Monica is as much the adventurer as I am. Some people will say that they have a great marriage because their partner balances them out. The wife is really bold and adventurous but the husband is more conservative, so together, they figure, they make a great team. I think Monica and I are accomplishing great things in life because there's no evening out. We're both comfortable living on the edge, and that's where great things happen.

This all works because we have a really strong marriage. Our margins may run thin elsewhere, but in terms of our relationship, there are deep reserves. We feel we have something really, really special.

Talking openly about our marriage can be awkward, in part because we are so accustomed to hearing people talk about the difficulties of marriage. When Monica and I were married someone came to our wedding and gave us a card that read, "It's hard, but just stick with it." For us, marriage has never been hard.

We both understand that marriage is a commitment, but is marriage just a commitment to be miserable?

"Just stick with it..."

Our lifestyle choices have affected our marriage. If you are married or planning to marry, understanding how your lifestyle choices will affect this primary relationship is pretty darn important.

I can't even begin to tell you how many men have confided in me that they'd _____ [FILL IN THE BLANK] if their wife would *let* them. I can't tell you how many women have confided in me that they'd _____ [FILL IN THE BLANK] if their husband would *let* them. It's sad to me because in each case I see people who aren't on the same page. They want different things in life. They don't have a shared vision.

Monica and I are often asked whose idea it was to embark on this quest to work less, live more, and travel the world as a family. Who first thought about the idea of patchwork income? Who first began re-thinking what our kids' educations would look like? Neither of us have any idea who had any of those ideas first. The ideas evolved in each of our minds together. The ideas have come and are coming to fruition in our collective mind and psyche.

There's been a lot of wine, too.

◆

IN VINO VERITAS.

It may sound humorous to suggest that you can find grand life truths in a bottle of wine, but I think there may be more to the idea than just a laugh. While Monica and I were dating and after we were married and in all the years since we have shared a lot of good conversations about our life and what we want life to look like. We've dreamed, often over a bottle of wine. We've thrown out ideas and then thrown them out (as in discarding them). We've gone on walks and we've gone on trips and we've had long dinners and we've... talked. We've talked a lot. All that talking is what has allowed us to remain so connected despite such radical changes in our life.

I can see how couples drift apart. After years and years of each going to work and living separate lives, how can you not drift at some point? If you're both working and then throw kids into the mix and try to keep up not only with their schedules but the pressures of modern Western culture, when do you have time to talk?

When do you have time to dream together?

When do you have time to be one?

There's a reason why there are so many affairs amongst people who are doing business together. There's a reason pastors have affairs with their assistants. It's because we become emotionally connected to the people we work with.

Work is emotional. There are frustrations and triumphs. There's a struggle, and a coming through the struggle toward victory. There's drama and intrigue and adventure. How can you not get all emotionally wrapped up with the person you are experiencing these things with? I get to experience those things with my wife everyday. It's powerful. Our work brings us closer together.

My wife is my partner in love and in life. She is my partner in loving and raising and being the primary educators of our kids. She's my business partner. She is my lover. In all areas of life she is my partner. Because of this, this question about which individual first had an idea sounds strange to us.

We're holding hands. As we walk through life, occasionally one of us may get a step ahead of their other. Subconsciously, at that moment, the one who is ahead will slow down. Or the opposite may be true: the person who is behind may catch up. We are always holding hands, though. It is impossible to get too far ahead or too far behind the other when you are holding hands.

My wife and I have partnered together to do some pretty cool things. This life that we're living is amazing. We're pulling it off together.

In January of 2008 I was poised to quit my job at the Reagan Ranch. My boss was flying into Santa Barbara from Washington, D.C. and I had arranged to have dinner with him the next evening. My resignation letter was ready. The night before, my wife and I were talking about what I was about to do.

I said, "I don't know, should I go through with this?"

She said, "What do you mean?"

I said, "I mean what if we can't make enough money?"

She said, "If it's the money, quit."

In other words, she said, "I want to be married to a man who's alive. If you stay in that job just for the money you're going to die. Not physically. But you're going to die. I need you. Not money. Not possessions. Not status. I need you."

One of my favorite songs, Chasing Cars by Snow Patrol, goes like this: "Forget what we're told, before we get too old, show me a garden that's bursting into life... All that I am, all that I ever was, is here in you perfect eyes, they're all I can see."

You'll notice a longing voice from Snow Patrol when they sing, "I need your grace to remind me to find my own." My wife helped me to find my own and I have helped her find her own. Alone, we could't have done this. Together, we have done amazing things.

◆

WE HAVE SEX ALL THE TIME. NO, REALLY...

Of course, there are less-than-amazing things my wife and I partner together to do, like vacuuming the house or changing diapers or putting in a few hours at the computer to take care of business. We have lots of long nights where we're both working at our computers. We challenge each other, push each other, and make demands of each other. We go to bed late, deal with the kids as they get up in the night, and ro-sham-beaux to see who gets to sleep in in the morning. We fold laundry and go to the grocery store.

That stuff, as mundane as it may seem, further connects us too. Studies show that couples where both partners are engaged in work outside the home and who share household responsibilities have more sex. I'm not sure which comes first - sharing household responsibilities creating good vibes or sharing household responsibilities growing out of a shared life. Whichever it is, who's going to argue with more sex?

If you've hit a rough patch in your marriage am I suggesting more sex?

Maybe I am.

Are you emotionally and spiritually connected because you have sex? Or do you have sex because you are emotionally and spiritually connected? I think it all works in tandem. Couples who are happy and connected have more sex. The more sex they have, the happier they become. I'm not saying the kind of connectivity my wife and I have or a great sex life is only possible by designing life the way we have. For us, though, it sure helps. I mean it's hard to argue with success, right?

Sure, we get frustrated with one another, have miscommunications, and can sometimes be downright irritable (usually me, not Monica). We get into funks. We go through times when we feel less connected. That's the exception, though.

Nothing will bring more joy into your life than a great marriage and nothing will make you more miserable in life than a lousy marriage. So it sure does seem worth considering how your life choices will impact your marriage.

There's a lot at stake.

That's why we talk.

What if you and your spouse don't have a shared vision?

Two partners talking about their future when they don't have a shared vision may actually end up being frustrating. So as much as I like talking, maybe talking isn't what you need... yet.

Instead, just do stuff. Be together. Experience life together. Re-arrange life to allow yourself to spend more time together. Turn off the TV. Put away your phones. Read the same books. Watch thought-provoking movies together. Go on a trip. Hold hands.

The most important thing Monica and I have is a shared vision. Our vision isn't now what it was when we first got married. Our vision changed, but that happened slowly, for both of us, together. We've talked about our vision while honeymooning at the Four Seasons and dropping thousands of dollars on weekend getaways in San Francisco and we've talked about our vision while selling stuff from around our house to buy groceries and while living in the in-laws garage.

When I was in high school I came across a quote that really impacted me. I scribbled it in a notebook and determined then that when I would someday have a wife I would look not just for someone who was beautiful or someone I had fun with but someone I could have a shared vision with. It's a line from Antoine de Saint-Exupery: *"Love does not consist in gazing at each other, but in looking outward together in the same direction."*

The vision may change, but for us, that's something that happens, together, as a couple. When you're holding hands, your eyes tend to fall in the same place.

When we were married, we had this Scripture from the book of Ecclesiastes read at our wedding. So far, it's proven to be true.

Two are better than one, because they have a good return for their labor:
If one falls down, his friend can lift him up.
But pity the man who falls and has no one to help him up!
Also, if two lie down together, they will keep warm.
Buy how can one keep warm alone?
Though one may be overpowered, two can defend themselves.
And a cord of three strands is not easily broken.

The Big Take-Aways

If you're single but have a mind to not be single one day, obviously, this is a pretty important topic. People give all kinds of advise when it comes to finding a mate. They'll tell you to find someone who makes you laugh or someone you have fun with. That advice is okay as far as it goes, but it doesn't go very far. Choose someone you share a vision with and someone you can talk with.

If you are already in a committed relationship, remember, "A house divided against itself cannot stand." Is your house divided? Do you and your partner share a vision? If not, commit to increasingly being of one mind. Have more shared experiences. Keep the conversation going. Share life together. Talk about what you're thinking and what you're feeling all the time. Eat, Talk, Make Love.

Action Steps

1. Make a chart and a weekly calendar to track how much time you actually spend with your partner. Do this for a few weeks without any variation in your typical routines to establish a baseline. Then think about how you can spend more time together.

2. Have a weekly dinner where you talk about vision. You can go out, or just do this at home. My wife and I often make ourselves a nice dinner at home that we have after the kids go to bed. With the fancy dishes out and a bottle of wine we tend to linger at the table a little longer. Talk about your evolving vision and make these discussions regular. Every idea is a possibility and entertain all ideas, at least for a time.

3. Take an honest look at your marriage. Where are you on the "Together Scale"? If you're not happy with your honest answer to this question, take action. Turn off the TV. Put

away your phones. Read the same books.
Watch thought-provoking movies together.
Go on a trip.

"My child arrived just
        the other day
He came to the world in
        the usual way
But there were planes to catch,
        and bills to pay
He learned to walk
        while I was away
And he was talking
        'fore I knew it,
        and as he grew
He'd say, "I'm gonna be
        like you, dad
You know I'm gonna
        be like you"

                Harry Chapin,
           Cat's in the Cradle

CHAPTER 11

Family > Career

In the weeks before my wife gave birth to our first baby I spent two days with two remarkable, highly accomplished men. Each said something to me that I'll never forget.

The first man told me how much my life was about to change. Lots of people had said those exact same words to me, but there was a glow about him as he said it. This was a man who'd been very successful in business and had built a global company that did billions of dollars in business each year. He was impressive, but it wasn't so much the business he had built that impressed me.

Looking back, I think what impressed me most was the way this man sought to live an examined life. He had been successful in business, but he knew there was more to life than business. And when he told me how much my life was about to change, his glow communicated how much he loved being a dad. Being a dad had actually changed his life.

A few days later, I spent time with someone who had achieved success in academia. I still remember our exact location on the road when we were in the car together and stopped at a stoplight. He made the motion with his hands as if he was holding a baby and said that when he held his baby for the first time he thought to himself, "I realize now how much my parents love me."

Weeks later, at Santa Barbara Cottage Hospital, my wife gave birth to our son Jackson. I sent text messages to both of those remarkable men I'd spent time with in the previous weeks and told them that my life had changed.

In the wee hours of the morning after my wife gave birth, Jackson went off to the nursery while Monica and I both tried to get some sleep. A short while later, a doctor came in and awakened us. He needed to talk to us about our son. Jackson was being transferred to the NICU. I tried to process what was being said, but the doctor told us that everything was fine and that we should go back to sleep. The next morning I learned what those letters -- NICU -- meant. Neonatal Intensive Care Unit.

Jackson had meconium aspiration and was having difficulty breathing. Looking back, it seems obvious to me now that he was going to be okay. At the time, I just remember being terrified.

One week after he was born, he was home with us.

Two months after I became a dad, I quit my job.

Thus was created this stark dividing line in my life. In the period of a few months I would go through two experiences that would change my life.

I didn't quit my job to become a stay-at-home dad. Jackson's birth was a powerful experience in my life, but I don't want to overstate what was going on. His entry into our world certainly sparked a lot of reflection about the way our lives were organized. I had a great job and I did have a lot of latitude in my job, but there were also times that my job could be very demanding, both in terms of the pressure being placed on me and my schedule. I was stressed out.

I did not quit to embrace the life that we have now. We were still a long way off from that. I quit my job to build a business and had no illusions as to how difficult a task that would be. I was expecting long hours. We were evaluating our life; to say we were going to completely reinvent our life at that time would be an exaggeration.

In the first months after I quit my job I was not working a lot. I was trying to move things forward, but there was only so much I could do everyday. I had work to do, but overall my schedule was really flexible.

In those months I got used to leisurely mornings at home and breakfast as a family. Being with my wife and my son all throughout the day became normal for me. My work became just another thing that I did, not the thing that I did. It wasn't like I went to work, did that for eight or nine or ten hours and then came home to be a family man. My life was now all jumbled together now. Feeding the baby one minute. Working on an important email the next. Having lunch with my wife later. Going to a business meeting in the afternoon. My life wasn't compartmentalized.

This schedule that became our daily modus operandi I viewed only as a season; it wasn't something I thought I could do long-term, I thought. Eventually, the deal I was working on would come together, and I would be putting in the long hours required in a staring and running a business.

Then the deal fell through. While my season of being at home was extended, I still viewed this time as a short-term season. I was working as a consultant now with an eye toward building a big firm. While I was able to enjoy time with my family as a one-man-show consultant, what I really saw myself doing was being a CEO. I'd fly all over the country and manage dozens of clients. I remember long walks with Monica during this season of our life, Jackson in the stroller or a baby carrier and us... talking. We talked about how I would organize an office, the things I would focus on and the things I would get other people to focus on. Heck, we talked about the decor of my future office. We talked about everything.

Then something happened.

Time passed and my priorities changed. I found myself less inter-ested in making more money and more interested in being a dad. Slowly the chase for a new career or business opportunity or more money began to take a back seat to lifestyle. You know all those stories you hear about guys at the end of their life reflecting about what they wish they'd done differently?

Wishing they'd spent more time with their family

Wishing they'd traveled more or gone camping more with their family

Wishing they'd been with their son when he took his first solo turns on skis

Wishing they'd taught their daughter how to dance

Wishing they'd taken the time to read more bedtime stories

That's not going to be me.

There are bills to be paid, sure. You have to pay the mortgage or the rent. You have to put food on the table and gas in the tank. The kids need clothes and shoes. I need a drink after we get the kids to bed.

I've chosen, though, to not make the chase for the bigger house in a better neighborhood or a second car, or a desire for any other material possession to rob me of the most valuable thing I can imagine: time with my kids.

It's not always easy. There are long days when my wife and I are juggling the kids and professional responsibilities and I think about how much easier life would be if I could just escape all day, five days a week and collect a paycheck.

There is an ebb and flow to our work. When I sit back and think about it, I really like this approach. We tend to batch a lot of our work in the spring and fall, leaving summer and winter to be more free. When we're cranking on work, it's easy to lose perspective, to forget that although we're working a lot now, in a few months we may only be working a few hours a week. It's easy to forget that the reason I'm up until one in the morning working on something is because I was snuggling on the couch with my kids until lunch time.

◆

TEACHING OUR KIDS ABOUT EXCHANGE RATES

Our lifestyle choices lead to a lot of questions about our family life and how our choices affect our kids. Recently, I was having lunch with a friend and we were talking about this idea that whatever we have in life we have because we traded part of our life to get it. The question is not whether or not I can afford something, the question is whether or not it's a good trade. Is the item in question something I am wiling to spend my life energy on?

My friend asked me if, when I am out with my kids and they ask me to buy them something, if I say, "I'm not willing to give my life for that toy."

Yes, actually I do.

I don't put it in quite the same words. But my wife and I talk a lot about life exchange rates with our kids. When they ask for something that's not in our budget or does not make sense to buy, I'll say something like, "No, we're not going to get that today. We're saving our money to go to Central America." I'm teaching my kids that life is all about choices.

I was on a walk with my daughter Emery when she was four-years-old and we saw a house with a three car garage. Emery really thought a three car garage was interesting and we talked about why a house would have a three car garage. She said it must be because they have three cars.

"But we have a two car garage, Emery," I said to her. "Do you think that we should get a second car since we have a two car garage?" Emery was convinced that yes, we should indeed get a second car.

"Well, Emery," I said. "Cars cost a lot of money. So if we get a second car we may not be able to go to Disneyland." Suddenly, Emery felt very differently about getting a second car.

When my kids ask me to buy them a toy, they need to understand lots of little decisions add up and if we get that toy, we don't get to go to the Rain Forest.

In preparing for our trip to Thailand, Monica and I were frequently talking about different items we could sell to add to our Thailand fund. One day, Emery came out of her room with some shoes that didn't fit anymore and said, "We can sell these so we have money to go to Thailand."

I'm really proud that my kids get this.

We have the same approach with our kids when we talk about work. Work isn't just what we do. My kids don't think I go to work just because I go to work.

So when I need to spend a few hours working and my kids want to play, Monica may say, "Daddy needs to work right now," to which our daughter may reply, "No, I don't want daddy to go to work." But when we tell her that I have to go to work so that I can make money so that we can go to Disneyland, she's okay with me going to work for a few hours. My work as a consultant to non-profit organizations requires me to travel on a regular basis. My wife recently overheard our daughter telling a friend, "My only hope to go to Disneyland is that my dad will go on a trip by himself for four days and make a lot of money."

When we're out and about, the kids don't always get the things they ask for, but I also don't just say, "no." And when they ask why, I don't say, "because I said so." I give them a reason. I give them something they can think about in a way that they can understand it. I'm trying to teach them about exchange rates and that we can have whatever we want in life, as long as we know what we want.

Robert Kiyosaki, the author of *Rich Dad Poor Dad* and many other excellent personal finance books points out that one big difference between rich families and poor ones is that rich parents talk to their kids about money all the time. They talk about how much they make and how they are investing it. They talk business at the dinner table. When these kids grow up, they know how to handle money. Poor kids don't. We are trying to do this with our kids, but more about how money relates to lifestyle. We talk about how if we buy something now, we may not have the money for something we want more later. Talking to kids early and often about how you spend your money, how you make money, and the proper role of money in our lives will help them have a healthy perspective on money as adults.

Sometimes, I give in and I give them what they're asking for. I reserve that right.

Our kids probably have fewer toys than most American kids their age. I think that fewer toys helps develop their creativity. And because we did not spend our money on toys, they got to go to the rain forest. For his birthday when he turned five, our son rode a horse to the top of a volcano and roasted marshmallows on cooling lava. How many kids get to do that?

We ski with our kids all winter long. We're at the beach with them all summer. We go on hikes and bike rides and spend months on the road together, camping and crashing in hotels and doing cannon balls in the pool. There's trips to the aquarium and the zoo and the museum, not occasionally, but all the time. There's trips to Central America and Thailand and lots of other amazing places. How many kids get to celebrate their 5th birthday roasting marshmellows over cooling lava? Our kids have ridden elephants, fed pink dolphins, and snorkeled the Andaman Sea. They've learn to count to 10 in Thai from a barkeep in Koh Samui. Their worldview, and mine, have been stretched by these amazing experiences.

This is possible for our family because of the way my wife and I have designed our life. We didn't get lucky. We did not win the lottery. We don't have a rich uncle.

We just know what we want.

◆

TOGETHER, WORKING AS HARD AS THREE QUARTERS OF ONE PERSON

We are deliberate.

Together, my wife and I are trying to work as hard as 3/4's the average person.

What do I mean by this?

A lot of families try to live on a single income. Usually, this means that one person in the relationship has a job outside the home while the other person manages the home and the family. My wife and I, though, both enjoy being engaged in work outside the home and we both enjoy being engaged in the home and as parents.

So we both share responsibilities in terms of income and in terms of managing the home and our family. We also want to make sure that we're not two ships passing in the night. If I work all day today while she takes care of the kids and she works all day tomorrow while I take care of the kids, that would be the equivalent of living on one income. We want to work less than that.

In the 1950's and 60's there were all sorts of predictions about how technology would soon allow us to work less and enjoy a better quality of life. All these years later, people are actually working more because our consumeristic impulses drive us to fill our lives with clutter. Working less and a better quality of life is possible now, you just have to figure out how to get rid of the clutter.

By together working as hard as three-quarters of the average person, we have time to each be engaged in work outside the home without our work controlling either one of us. The typical work week is 40 hours, so our goal would be that between the two of us, we would work no more than a combined 30 hours a week, leaving plenty of time for other activities in our lives.

There have been times that one of us has to work a lot more. Sometimes we find ourselves buried in a project. There are weeks that we put in a combined 80 hours. During our three months in Thailand, I would estimate that we worked a combined total of about 60 hours, which averages out to about 5 hours a week. (That's pretty good, don't you think?) The goal is that over time we work no more than a combined 30 hours a week.

Our life does not revolve around our work. We're trying to teach or kids, in the words of George Mallory, the English schoolteacher and mountaineer who died trying to be the first to reach the summit of Mount Everest, that, *"We do not live to eat and make money. We eat and make money to be able to enjoy life."*

What does your lifestyle teach your kids? What values does your calendar communicate? The grind is normal. So are crappy marriages and disconnected parents. Be weird.

The Big Take-Aways

Your choices will impact your kids more than anyone else so why not involve them in the discussions about your life choices. As I said in the *Letter to my Children* at the beginning of this book, while Jean Luc Godard may have been right when he said that he who jumps into the void owes no explanation to those who stand and watch, I think I do owe some explanation to my kids.

I hope my kids appreciate my explanation. The time I get to spend with them is far more valuable than anything else. The two-year-old version of my son Jackson is gone forever. I can never get that kid back, so I want to enjoy every moment I can with each of my kids as they are growing up. I want to be with them now, when they need me most, instead of working hard now and then retiring to an empty home.

Action Steps

1. Commit to being open and honest with your kids. Don't hide behind a veil or think they can't handle financial issues.

2. Spend an evening talking about what your ideal family life would look like. School, daily routines, work, household chores, etc. and revisit this discussion regularly.

3. Have a garage sale and use the proceeds to fund a family adventure. Talk with your kids about the adventure you're going to go on and get everyone on board with the plan. Then start finding things to sale and ask your kids to also contribute items. When you're on your family adventure with the proceeds from the garage sale, ask your kids if they'd rather have the toys they got rid of or this great adventure. (Make sure you ask this question at a moment it's sure not to backfire!). You'll be teaching them that life is all about choices and trade-offs.

"Imagination is the source of every form of human achievement. And it's the one thing that I believe we are systematically jeopardizing in the way we educate our children and ourselves."

Sir Ken Robinson

CHAPTER 12

unSchooling + unWorking

My work is almost seamlessly intertwined into my life. When I am skiing, I go to the lodge to check my email and respond to messages. While I am on the chairlift, I often find myself in conversations that lead to me exchanging contact information with the person next to me. When I am at my computer, I'm pushing forward on a project, but I can't tell if it's business or personal. It doesn't feel like work, although I guess there are people who would say what I am doing looks like work. Wave, the program we use for our accounting is open, but so is Facebook.

For me, the line between what is recreation and what is work can often be very blurry. What's fun and what's work isn't defined by punching a time clock.

Why should it be any different for my kids? Why should I think that in order for them to learn, they have to be at a school? If I don't go to an office to work, why should they go to a school to learn?

Almost as soon as our son Jackson turned five, people began to ask questions about our schooling choices. At the time we were traveling in Central America and usually the questions came from curious twenty-something backpackers we met in the hostels where we bunked. We found our interactions rewarding because so often travelers shared that they never thought backpacking through Central America would be possible when they had a family. We were told over and over again by these twenty-somethings that we gave them hope. It was really special for us.

When people ask about school for our kids I often try to come up with the most outrageous answer possible, not because I'm trying to be a jerk, but because I want to get people to think differently than the way they've been taught to think.

Jackson and I may be riding up a chairlift or playing together in a hotel swimming pool when the friendly person next to us asks, "Where do you go to school?" I get a confused look when I say, "He's in school right now."

Our kids have been in school all their life. They didn't know anything when they were born! The world has been their classroom and Monica and I have been their teachers.

One of my favorite books is *A Pirate Looks at 50* by Jimmy Buffett. I know what you're thinking. You think I'm crazy because I'm taking advise on life and parenting from the guy who's wasting away in Margaritaville. The book is chock full of great advice on life and I'll take advice from a guy who understands that, "one of the inescapable encumbrances of leading an interesting life is that there have to be moments when you almost lose it."

In the book he tells a story about a trip to Costa Rica with his family and a hike he took with his kids to a waterfall.

"It had taken me thirty-three years to get to my first ocean-side wa-terfall. My kids had made it during their single digit years. That's what it's all about. They will be moving on before we know it, headed off to adolescence and adulthood like Savannah [Buffett's oldest daughter] before them. When they get there, I want them to have a sense of who they are and what the world they live in is really all about. I sit some-times in wonder, listening to parents in New York talk about the proper preschool that will enable their children to be best prepared for the primo kindergarten in the city. My God, I think. Is this what's best for the kids, or is it about what the parents missed out on in their childhood? The rewarding part of parenting is being able to share experiences with your children. The way I look at it, experience is the best teacher. There's plenty of time for my kids to adapt to whatever school situation they'll eventually find themselves in. But by the time they get there, they will have ridden elephants in Thailand, experienced G-forces in an airplane, learned to bait a hook and release a fish. And they will have swam neckie in a waterfall by the sea."

Like a lot of couples, when Monica and I were newlyweds we talk-ed about how we would eventually approach our kids' educations. Our thinking has come a long, long way since those theoretical dis-cussions. Slowly, our views on how we would educate our kids came in line with our views on work and how we are designing our life.

This goes beyond the public/private debate. The idea that there's a difference between public and private is an illusion. This is about the entire education paradigm. With very few exceptions, public and private schools operate within the same paradigm. It's a paradigm that worked great for the early 20th century. It's a paradigm that needs to be shattered for education to meet the needs of the ~~emerging~~ already here world.

If you're not ready to buy into my suggestion that school (public and private) is broken then Seth Godin's book, *Stop Stealing Dreams (WHAT IS SCHOOL FOR)* is a book you simply must read.

Here's section three of his manifesto, which he titled *Back to (the wrong) school*:

A hundred and fifty years ago, adults were incensed about child labor. Low-wage kids were taking jobs away from hard-working adults.

Sure, there was some moral outrage about seven-year-olds losing fingers and being abused at work, but the economic rationale was paramount. Factory owners insisted that losing child workers would be catastrophic to their industries and fought hard to keep the kids at work—they said they couldn't afford to hire adults. It wasn't until 1918 that nationwide compulsory education was in place.

Part of the rationale used to sell this major transformation to industrialists was the idea that educated kids would actually become more compliant and productive workers. Our current system of teaching kids to sit in straight rows and obey instructions isn't a coincidence—it was an investment in our economic future. The plan: trade short-term child-labor wages for longer-term productivity by giving kids a head start in doing what they're told.

Large-scale education was not developed to motivate kids or to create scholars. It was invented to churn out adults who worked well within the system. Scale was more important than quality, just as it was for most industrialists.

Of course, it worked. Several generations of productive, fully employed workers followed. But now?

Nobel prize–winning economist Michael Spence makes this really clear: there are tradable jobs (doing things that could be done somewhere else, like building cars, designing chairs, and answering the phone) and non-tradable jobs (like mowing the lawn or cooking burgers). Is there any question that the first kind of job is worth keeping in our economy?

Alas, Spence reports that from 1990 to 2008, the U.S. economy added only 600,000 tradable jobs.

If you do a job where someone tells you exactly what to do, he will find someone cheaper than you to do it. And yet our schools are churning out kids who are stuck looking for jobs where the boss tells them exactly what to do.

Do you see the disconnect here? Every year, we churn out millions of workers who are trained to do 1925-style labor.

The bargain (take kids out of work so we can teach them to become better factory workers as adults) has set us on a race to the bottom. Some people argue that we ought to become the cheaper, easier country for sourcing cheap, compliant workers who do what they're told. Even if we could win that race, we'd lose. The bottom is not a good place to be, even if you're capable of getting there.

As we get ready for the ninety-third year of universal public education, here's the question every parent and taxpayer needs to wrestle with: Are we going to applaud, push, or even permit our schools (including most of the private ones) to continue the safe but ultimately doomed strategy of churning out predictable, testable, and mediocre factory workers?

As long as we embrace (or even accept) standardized testing, fear of science, little attempt at teaching leadership, and most of all, the bu-reaucratic imperative to turn education into a factory itself, we're in big trouble.

The post-industrial revolution is here. Do you care enough to teach your kids to take advantage of it?

I read *Stop Stealing Dreams* at a time when I was really starting to think deeply about education and it rocked my world. You can view, download to your tablet, or print Seth's entire manifesto in several formats at http://www.squidoo.com/stop-stealing-dreams

Sir Ken Robinson is an educator who has brought attention to the broken education paradigm through his massively popular Ted Talks. His lecture, "How Schools Kill Creativity" is the most viewed Ted Talk of all time. I would highly recommend Sir Ken Robinson as a resource to you if you are interested in re-thinking how we as a society do school.

Along with Seth Godin and Sir Ken Robinson, Monica and I have been greatly influenced and we are deeply indebted to a number of bloggers who have helped us sort though these ideas. Christina Pilkington who publishes the blog Interest Led Learning at http://christinapilkington.com has been a tremendous resource to us. Christina is a former teacher, who, when she became pregnant with her twins, decided to follow her instincts in the classroom and allow kids to spend the majority of their days on activities of their own choosing. Christiana had nothing to lose because she and her husband had decided that she would not return to the classroom when their twins were born. The results were amazing, yet school administrators were none too happy. She was told to be glad she was pregnant and leaving because she would not have been asked back.

"They didn't need 'my type' of teacher there," Christina recalls. She was messing with the paradigm.

Our friend Jennifer Miller from the blog The Edventure Project published at http://edventureproject.com has also been a great inspiration to us. Jennifer and her family have lived all over the world and approach life as an adventure and learning happens along the way. Knowing Jennifer, reading her blog and following her posts on Facebook has been inspiring and reassuring to us because her kids are older than ours and we've been able to observe that they are creative, articulate, thoughtful, caring kids. We've also followed Greg and Rachel Denning and even had an opportunity to spend a few days with them and their family at Lake Atitlan in Guatemala in 2012. We met up with the Dennigs at a time when we were being heavily influenced by the unschooling movement, but the Dennings have a much more rigorous, Jeffersonian approach with their older kids. Their influence was accentuated in our life at just the right time. You can find the Dennings at http://discovershareinspire. com/. Lainie Liberti from http://www.raisingmiro.com/ has been yet another influence among many, many more.

The point is, if you want to re-think education, you don't have to do it on your own. I don't line up perfectly with any of the people I've mentioned, but they've all inspired me and I've taken something from them. Even if your kids are in a more conventional school environment, I encourage you to check out the individuals I've mentioned here so you can incorporate some of their thinking in your family time with your kids. I'm critical of the education paradigm, but please don't read this as me saying your kids are doomed if you send them to school. As parents, we each do what we think is right for our kids. The most important thing for kids is that they have loving and involved parents.

◆

THE FUTURE IS NOW

Our culture once needed people to go to work, go into debt, and send their kids to school. That's not the future. Our education system is designed to train kids for a world that no longer exists.

The future is one of flexibility and customization. Freelance is a word we'll hear more and more. Monica and I are early adapters of the emerging world; we are ahead of the curve. Life will get easier for us not just because we'll get better at this life, but because the emerging world will accommodate us. We're weird now, but we're the future normal.

We want to give our kids an education that prepares them for the ~~emerging~~ already here world. Although our kids usually tell people they are homeschooled, and we use the term as well because it's vernacular people understand, we don't like the term homeschool because it implies we "do school" at home, which we don't.

There are lots of terms used by others like world-schooling, road-schooling, and unschooling. I'm not sure we neatly fit into any one category, nor do I feel that we need to. I love the term "hackschooling," which was coined by Logan LaPlante. His Ted Talk, *Hackschooling Makes Me Happy*, given when he was 13 years old, has more than eight million views on YouTube. In his talk, he asserts that when he grows up he wants to be happy.

"We don't seem to make learning how to be happy and healthy a priority in our schools," LaPlante says, "It's separate from schools. And for some kids, it doesn't exist at all. But what if we didn't make it separate? What if we based education on the study and practice of being happy and healthy, because that's what it is, a practice, and a simple practice at that."

Logan LaPlante is a Reno-Tahoe kid, and he's a skier. In his Ted Talk he identifies professional skier Shane McConkey as his hero, but not for the reason you may think:

"Shane McConkey is my hero. I loved him because he was the world's best skier. But then, one day I realized what I really loved about Shane; he was a hacker. Not a computer hacker, he hacked skiing. His creativity and inventions made skiing what it is today, and why I love to ski. A lot of people think of hackers as geeky computer nerds who live in their parent's basement and spread computer viruses, but I don't see it that way."

"Hackers are innovators, hackers are people who challenge and change the systems to make them work differently, to make them work better, it's just how they think, it's a mindset."

"I'm growing up in a world that needs more people with the hacker mindset and not just for technology, everything is up for being hacked, even skiing, even education. So whether it's Steve Jobs, Mark Zuckerberg or Shane McConkey, having the hacker mindset can change the world."

Logan LaPlante's entire Ted Talk is well worth the listen. You can find it on YouTube by searching "Hackschooling."

Whatever you want to call it, the idea is that learning and play should be seamless and maybe even indistinguishable.

It's exactly what we're seeking to do with our work. I believe that I'll do great work when I am doing work that I really love. I do my best work when it does not feel like work at all. My best work is play; it's unWorking. My kids get lost in learning because it's fun; it's unSchooling.

I can't think of a better way to educate my kids than to do exactly what we are doing: allow them to go through life with us, explore, travel, try new things, ask questions and go wherever their interests take them. We travel. We read books. We go to the grocery store. We talk about money and how we make money and budgets. The best preparation for real life is real life.

unSchooling and unWorking does not happen from seven to three or eight to five. Our lives are filled with learning, work and play from the moment we wake up to the moment we lay our heads down to sleep. It's just life.

This approach to education is the most exciting and the most exhausting thing I have ever experienced. It would be easier, perhaps, to have a curriculum and to sit down at the dining room table every day at a set time and "do school." Instead, we find ourselves at the BTS Sky Train Station in Bangkok, chaos surrounding us, and we're helping the kids read the map. We can't get on the train until they know where we are, where we're going, and how much money we'll need to get there. Once that's figured out we have to go to the cashier to change our paper money for coins and we have to count it out for each member of our family. A simple process of paying our fare and loading a train that could take me 10 seconds we spend 10 minutes figuring out as a family. Look at what the kids have done, though. They've read a map, they've done some math, they've handled money, and they've had to interact with other people to accomplish their goals.

Our mission as parents in regards to the education of our kids is to raise resourceful, respectful, curious kids who love learning and can adapt to a changing world, empowering them to lead happy and healthy lives.

The future of work is unWorking; we're educating our kids today for a world they'll live in tomorrow. Don't get stuck in the last century and don't leave your kids there either. This is work and education in the ~~emerging~~ already here world.

The Big Take-Aways

Our world has changed, but the way we view both work and school has not changed.

If you're into this whole idea of re-inventing your life and you have kids... don't forget to re-invent their life too. If you're trying to escape the grind, don't put your kids in their own grind. Get your kids out of the minaturied, pressurized rat race. Even if your kids are in a more conventional school setting, you can still incorporate these principles in your family time.

Our goal is to lead happy, healthy lives and to sustain a love for learning. This is also our goal for our kids and these things are not taught in school. We believe that our approach to work is the way of the future. By modeling our kids' schooling and education after our approach to work, we believe we are best preparing them for their futures.

Action Items

1. Think about the real goals of education for your kids. Write a mission statement centered around those goals. Our mission in regards to the education of our kids is to raise resourceful, respectful, curious kids who love learning and can adapt to a changing world, empowering them to lead happy and healthy lives. Once you have your mission statement, evaluate how well your kids current education model serves your goals. We've decided that standardized tests don't help us meet our goals.

2. Think about how getting your kids out of the the grind would free you up to live more fully. What kind of freedom would you have? What would you do with that freedom? What might your kids learn from that?

"Life is either a daring adventure or nothing at all."

Helen Keller

CHAPTER 13

Go a little crazy

On April 11, 2009, an unemployed, 47-year-old woman with a cheeky grin walked onto the stage of the hit UK show *Britain's Got Talent*. Her dream, she told the judges, thousands in attendance and millions watching at home, was to be a professional singer.

The raised eyebrows and snickers from the judges and studio audience did not deter her. I'm sure she was well accustomed to both, but Susan Boyle was crazy enough to keep pursuing her dream.

That night, on *Britain's Got Talent*, Susan Boyle stunned a nation. Her performance of *I Dreamed a Dream* from *Les Miserables* was absolutely breathtaking. Within nine days, videos of Susan Boyle's audition as well as other footage of the unassuming woman from Scotland had been viewed online more than 100 million times.

What was it about Susan Boyle that touched the world so deeply?

Why such an overwhelming reaction?

Go to YouTube and search for Susan Boyle's first appearance on *Britain's Got Talent*. There are a few moments I want to draw to your attention. Not deterred by the disbelief of the audience and judges, when the music starts playing and just before she starts singing, Susan Boyle gets a little smirk on her face. She can feel it. This is her moment.

She starts to sing and the crowd comes to their feet. Susan Boyle opens up. She's rising to the occasion. She's singing beautifully. The judges know this song. Many of the people in the audience know this song. Those who know this song know a very difficult part of the song -- a part that very few singers can pull off -- is now approaching. Will she pull it off? She nails it. As she comes into the home stretch, the music continues while there's a pause in the singing. Susan Boyle smiles at the judges and then sings the last lines of the song directly looking at the judges. She knows she's done it. There's no record deal yet, but she's already achieved her dream.

People identified with Susan Boyle. Among the now 200 million people who have viewed videos of her debut performance on YouTube, there are no doubt many who are presently pursuing their dreams. There are also, no doubt, many who have buried their dream deep within. Whichever the case is for you, I suspect you recognized Susan Boyle when you saw her doing her little victory dance on stage.

Is there a Susan Boyle in you?

◆

REVIVING THE DREAMER

When we're kids, dreaming comes naturally. Our imaginations run wild and everything is possible. Over time, our schools and our consumerist culture beat the dreamer into submission. We're taught to think according to career counselors. We begin thinking less about what we love or what we were born to do and more about meeting market demands or how much money we can make at a profession.

We're taught having fun is selfish and irresponsible. We must be practical, resourceful, dutiful. Art and music are wonderful hobbies, but we need to get a job and be constructive. At an early age, the dreamer begins to die and the settler emerges.

I'm a chairlift chatterbox. When I'm skiing and it comes time to get on a chairlift, I talk it up to the person sitting next to me. The conversation I had with the Netflix executive was not unusual. It was only interesting because of his connection to Netflix. I have similar conversations all the time and everyone wants to know how to move to Tahoe. Moving to Tahoe is easy. The hard part is reviving the dreamer who'll actually do it.

When I ask someone, "Ideally, what would you want life to look like?" even if they don't use these words, what they're often thinking is, "I'd like to make a lot of money." People associate money with freedom and conversely, freedom with money.

Money is an easy solution if you find yourself in possession of a winning lottery ticket. Without a winning lottery ticket or some stroke of luck, money is a very hard solution because in order to get money we have to trade a part of our life. When people say, "It's just money..." they are absolutely wrong. It's not just money, it's life energy.

When I ask the question, "What would you like your life to look like?," most people picture themselves making more money or having more vacation time or having more of both.

So instead of taking a weekend ski trip they could take a week long ski trip and instead of staying in a cheap hotel they could stay in one of the beautiful condos on the slopes. But the answer to the *"What do you want life to look like?"* question almost always comes back to time and money. Few people think about completely overhauling their life.

It's like life is a highway and the only question is how nice of a car they can afford. There's more than one way to travel and there are lots of side roads and shortcuts.

I'd like to talk to the 13-year-old version of a lot of the people I ride with on chairlifts. Tell a 13-year-old kid, *"You may not make as much money, but you'll be happy. You'll be able to live in the mountains and have more leisure time instead of working long hours and being stuck in traffic two times a day five times a week. You'll be able to ski as much as you want and when you have kids of your own, you'll be able to spend time with them and have fun."*

No 13-year-old kid would say, *"Nah, I'd rather live in LA and make five times as much money and spend all of it on an expensive apartment and a flashy car."*

It just does not happen!

Adults do it all the time, either by design or by default.

If your dream is to live in LA, go for it! But don't live in LA and trade your life for all those dollars and then trade all those dollars for an expensive apartment and a flashy car if you've never even determined that's what you want in life. Maybe your dream is to live in the city and to conquer the business world. That's great! Go for it! Take the time to figure out what you want. Align your life with your values. If you're not mindful about these kinds of decisions, a plethora of addictions await you.

For me, journaling has been an invaluable tool for carving out my dream. Taking the time to go back and read things I wrote two or three or ten or fifteen years ago has always had a way of bringing me back to myself. Skiing is an escape for me, it's a time for me to clear my head. I love going on hikes because of the opportunity to think. There's no media to distract me, only nature and my heart. When Monica and I want to talk, we'll often make a really nice dinner, the kind that leads you linger at the table a little longer. I also enjoy cigars and one thing I love about a cigar is that it's kind of like an hourglass. When I am smoking a cigar, I don't expose myself to media -- it's just me and my cigar -- and I know that I am going to sit, relax and think until the cigar is done.

When I was "successful" in my career, the idea of skiing 60 days a year seemed impossible. Spending six weeks in Central America, let alone three months in Thailand, seemed like something reserved only for millionaires. The only way I could have imagined such a scenario would have been to work really hard and save a lot of money so that maybe I could retire early and do it then.

It's a whole lot easier to move to Tahoe and just figure it out.

It's not about the money, it's about the life.

I think the 13-year-old me would be proud.

What would the 13-year-old you think of you today?

◆

LIVE RIDICULOUSLY

"That's how you become great, man. Hang your balls out there."

It's a slightly crass way of saying something completely true.

Greatness is never achieved with timidity.

In the movie *Jerry Maguire*, the title character played by Tom Cruise is a successful sports agent working at a large firm representing some of the most highly paid athletes in the world. He has a sick feeling that there's more to life and even more to business than the money. He stays up all night typing on his laptop a mission statement for the future of his company.

Jerry says, "Hey, I'll be the first to admit it. What I was writing was somewhat *touchy feely*. I didn't care. I had lost the ability to bullshit. It was the me I'd always wanted to be." In the middle of the night he drives to a Copy Max and has his manifesto professionally printed and bound. The attendant hands him a copy for review and says, "That's how you become great, man. Hang your balls out there."

Within a matter of days, Jerry is fired.

In his book *The Hypomanic Edge*, psychologist John Gartner writes about the link between manic behavior and some of the most successful entrepreneurs of the past decade. What does it mean to be hypomanic? Well, hypo means just below, as in just below the threshold of something. Add manic, and we're talking about being just below the threshold of crazy.

That's right. Some of the most successful entrepreneurs of the past decade have been just on the edge of crazy. If you have followed some of the stories about these people, I'm sure you agree. Steve Jobs was just on the edge of crazy. The edge of crazy is a really creative spot and manics are just crazy enough to push forward their crazy ideas. Hence, Pixar. Hence, Apple.

But this hypomanic behavior is not reserved just for entrepreneurs like Steve Jobs.

Hypomanics are lifestyle designers. I know hypomanics who've left "secure" corporate jobs to move to the mountains and other hypomanics who've sold all their earthly possessions to set off on a quest to travel forever. I know hypomanics who've cycled from Alaska to Argentina with their twin nine-year-old boys.

I too am a hypomanic.

If you've ever been sharing your plans with someone and they've said to you, "You're crazy..." chances are, you're a hypomanic too. Hypomanics do what they love, regardless of how crazy the idea may seem to some. Hypomanics are innovators. In business, technology, music, art, fashion, culture, and every other field under the sun, hypomanics make us richer. They make the world more beautiful. If you read stories about tremendous athletes like Michael Jordan or Peyton Manning, you'll probably find yourself saying, "That's a little crazy." That's because Michael Jordan and Peyton Manning are hypomanics.

In the summer of 2001 I drove across the United States with my friend Todd. We were heading to Santa Barbara where I was about to begin living what was then very much the life of my dreams. We stopped to crash for the night in Breckenridge, Colorado and I told Todd that night that I had this weird feeling that I was going to have a little *Jerry Maguire* in my life.

I was moving to Santa Barbara and my life was going exactly as planned. Still, I had this suspicion that at some point I'd go a little crazy.

Actually, I knew it.

In *Jerry Maguire* the audience watches Jerry slowly lose all of his financial success. Then, one day, we see that he's moved out of his trendy apartment and into his sister-in-law's house. The film doesn't portray the actual move. It doesn't cut to scenes of what was actually going on with Jerry as that was all going down. We don't see him packing up his apartment into cardboard boxes. I don't need to see that on the screen because I know exactly what that looks like. I've lived it.

You know how Jerry seems while he's living in his sister-in-law's house? He seems happy. He's smiling. He seems okay with it. We're shown that Jerry was happier living in his sister-in-law's house than he would have been if he'd just towed the corporate line and stayed in that "safe" and successful job.

That's how you become great, man. You hang your balls out there.

Jerry Maguire lost everything and realized losing everything isn't that bad.

Go a little crazy and make your 13-year-old self proud.

The Big Take-Aways

You once had a dream. Somewhere along the way you buried your dream to meet society's expectations. Remember that exchange from the movie *Up in the Air*:

Ryan Bingham: I'm not a shrink, Bob, I'm a wake up call. You know why kids love athletes?

Bob: I don't know, because they screw lingerie models...

Ryan Bingham: No, that's why we love athletes. Kids love athletes because they followed their dreams.

Bob: Well I can't dunk.

Ryan Bingham: No, but you can cook.

Bob: What are you talking about?

Ryan Bingham: Your resume says you minored in French Culinary Arts. Most students work the frier at KFC. You bused tables at Il Picatorre to support yourself. Then you got out of college and started working here. How much did they pay you to give up on your dreams?

Bob: Twenty seven grand a year.

Ryan Bingham: At what point were you going to stop and go back to what made you happy?

When are you going to stop and go back to what makes you happy?

Society has labeled certain aspirations as ridiculous because they don't make a lot of money. They aren't ridiculous if your goal is happiness and fulfillment. Re-think your definition of success. If others think you're crazy, remember that a little crazy isn't a bad thing. Successful people are able to block out the noise and the naysayers.

Action Steps

1. If you've kept journals throughout your life, dig up your old ones and read them.

2. Talk with your partner about crazy ideas you've had that you've never acted on. Why haven't you?

3. Take on the mind of the thirteen year old you and write a letter to yourself. What do you think of yourself? How is the thirteen year old you disappointed? What makes the thirteen year old you proud?

"I'm not afraid to die
I'm not afraid to live
And when I'm flat on my back
I hope to feel like I did."

U2, Kite

CHAPTER 14

Live Epicly Now

When I first moved to Santa Barbara I lived in an area of town called the Mesa. I loved living on the Mesa. We had our own little community within Santa Barbara -- a grocery store, pizza place, ice cream parlor, a couple of bars and a few places to grab a meal. On Saturdays I could drop off my dry cleaning and walk a few doors down to Mesa Barbers and get a haircut while talking sports. From my living room and the front deck of my house I could look out at the Pacific Ocean. It was idyllic.

My house was just a few miles from where I worked and there were two main routes I could take to get there. The first and most logical way to go would have been to take Cliff Drive all the way down into town. It was a straight shot and once I turned onto Cliff Drive from my house, I would not need to turn again. I'd drive straight until I pulled to the side of the road to park my car. The second route was slightly longer and meandered along the Pacific coast on Shoreline Drive.

A coworker who also lived on the Mesa asked me if I took Shoreline Drive into work everyday. I didn't. That route on Cliff Drive was so easy I never thought about going any other way. My colleague's eyes glazed over as he described the feeling of driving into work everyday on Shoreline Drive. It was worth the extra few minutes to him because of the way it made him feel.

The next morning I got in my car, put the top down, and drove into work along the Pacific Ocean on Shoreline Drive. I took the same route every time I drove to work until years later when Monica and I bought our first home and moved off of the Mesa.

That act -- driving a few minutes out of my way -- was a simple way to live epicly. Choosing the scenic route was a simple way for me to make the very most out of my situation in life.

Santa Barbara is one of the most beautiful places in the world to live. It's also one of the most expensive. Yet I talk with people all the time in Santa Barbara who are not experiencing the best that Santa Barbara had to offer. They are not maximizing their investment in Santa Barbara. They aren't sucking the marrow out of life. They could be living anywhere. They are living their lives as if they are in a windowless apartment, but they are paying Santa Barbara prices to live there.

Babe Ruth was once asked about his strategy for hitting home runs. He said, "I swing as hard as I can and I try to swing right through the ball... I swing big, with everything I've got. I hit big or I miss big. I like to live as big as I can."

. lived in Santa Barbara I sought out all of the best that .rbara had to offer. I went to cultural festivals and hiked ᴀ the foothills. I went to the beach, got to know wine country anᴄ̣ ould hardly wait for the free "Concert in the Park" series to start each summer. Santa Barbara has the second highest person to restaurant ratio in the United States and I sampled my share of them and developed a list of favorites. And I drove along the Pacific Ocean on Shoreline Drive to work instead of taking the slightly shorter route.

Since moving to Lake Tahoe, I've discovered that Santa Barbara isn't the only place in the world where people often don't take advantage of the best their location has to offer. Winter is six months long. If you can't figure out a way to enjoy it, all you're doing is shoveling your driveway. I'm passionate about skiing, but not everyone has to ski. There's cross country skiing, or snowshoeing, or ice skating. The same is true in the summer. Our beaches along Lake Tahoe are magnificent. Yet every summer many locals spend less time at the beach than people who vacation here.

Wherever you live, make the most of it.

Live big. Live epicly.

When I tell people to live epicly, I think sometimes they hear me saying, "live like me." That's not what I'm suggesting. Make the most of *your* life, wherever *you* are, *right now*. Whatever you may want life to look like in the future, you can be that person today with every choice you make.

If you live in the mountains, enjoy the mountains. If you live at the beach, enjoy the beach. If you live in an incredible cultural center, enjoy the culture. Be interesting. This really goes beyond where we live and the recreation we choose. This is about our entire life energy and where we spend it and how we spend it.

You may think that the way your life looks today is simply a reaction to the circumstances you've encountered in situations beyond your control.

If that's the case, stop for a minute and don't even think about your dream life. Don't think about what your ideal life looks like. Instead, think about your life now. Think about what your life would look like now without any changes in your finances or your job or your relationships if you made the decision to live epicly now.

Until you're living epicly in the present, you're not ready for an epic future.

What does epic look like for you, right now, without any changes in the circumstances that are beyond your control?

My brother spent the second half of his 30s taking care of his sick wife, who passed away in 2013. While caring for his wife and dealing with the heartbreaking reality of the inevitable end, asking my brother, "what would your ideal life look like?" could only derive an answer beyond his control. Of course his ideal life would have included his wife being well, but he had no power to accomplish that. But asking, "how can you live epicly now?" is a different question.

For me, one the biggest ways I can live epicly now is to control my schedule. I'm self-employed and I do have to work, but the hours I work are very flexible. What I typically do most days, is get up first thing in the morning and do a few tasks, and then almost completely step away from work for the rest of the day, not returning until the sun is down and my kids are in bed.

There are a lot of disadvantages to being self-employed. I do not have a guaranteed paycheck. I don't have employer-provided health benefits and I don't get "paid time off." Because there are disadvantages, I want to maximize every advantage out there. So I do fun things while the sun is up and enjoy being with my kids and then I work at night. If I'm self-employed but I keep the same hours as the average employee, I now have all the drawbacks of being self-employed and have taken one of the benefits off of the table for myself.

That's what living epicly looks like for me.

What might it look like for you?

This is taking lifestyle design down to the basics. Rather than doing a demolition and starting from nothing, this is just a remodel. It's a new kitchen or a new bathroom. If you're interested in completely overhauling your life, this is a great way to train yourself how to live a life of your own design. If you're already seeking to live an examined life or you're well on the path of your reinvented life, this is a great way to make sure you don't fall into ruts and end up watching life pass you by.

Choose to live epicly. Now.

The Big Take-Aways

Life re-invention is scary. Carl Sandburg said, "Life is like an onion; you peel it off one layer at a time, and sometimes you weep."

Until you're willing to make changes in your present life -- today -- you're not ready for life re-invention. Make the most of where you are right now. Until you do this, you aren't ready to make the huge changes. Change your attitude about where you are right now. Take the scenic route. Make the most of the opportunities before you every single day.

Until you're living epicly in the present, you're not ready for an epic future.

Action Steps

1. Plan an EPIC day! Plan a day right where you're at and make the absolute most of it. Enjoy whatever the best of your community or corner of the world has to offer. Write a love letter. Have sex. Eat delicious food. Exercise. Live.

2. Plan an EPIC week! A day can feel like a vacation, but you don't want an epic vacation, you want an epic life. So plan a week that includes work and routines, things that you are passionate about, and.... Write a love letter. Have sex. Eat delicious food. Exercise. Live.

3. There may be some things that are outside of your control. The vast majority of us have far more power than we realize. Take out a piece of paper and create three columns. In the first column list everything that is completely outside of your control. In the second column list the things where you have

limited control, and in the third column list things where you have complete control and the power to change. Are you surprised at how weak you have been acting based upon how much power you actually possess? What does this mean for your future?

Exhortation

I live with regret.

I regret things that I've said and I regret the way that I've treated people. There have been times I've been a jerk. Other times, I was well-intentioned but just plain wrong. I've made mistakes and done things I would take back.

Let me tell you what I do not regret.

I do not regret my decision to quit my job.

I do not regret my decision to stay out of the traditional work force.

I do not regret going through the process of reinventing my life.

I do not regret all the kisses and cuddles I've had with my kids.

I do not regret all the skiing.

I do not regret all the travel.

I do not regret the margin I have in my life.

I do not regret the life I chose, and continue to choose every day.

Years ago, when we were in Tahoe at the beginning of our six-month cross-country road trip, we had one of those "what were we thinking?!?" days. We had come to Tahoe to enjoy the snow and it was raining. There is nothing more depressing than rain in a ski town.

We were driving around trying to figure out something to do. In the back of our minds, Monica and I were each thinking about how much easier it would be to be home in Santa Barbara. We were stuck. Our place was rented out and we couldn't go home for six months.

I turned to Monica and said in a depressed tone, *"this is the life we chose."*

A few days later, a cold front arrived packing plenty of precipitation. Lake Tahoe was blanketed in two feet of snow. We arranged for someone to babysit Jackson while Monica and I headed to Sierra-at-Tahoe Resort for a day of skiing. It was incredible. We rode the chairlift up to the top and Monica and I stood at the edge of the slope waiting to push off. I turned to her with a grin on my face said, *"this is the life we chose."*

We chose the difficulty of stepping out of our comfort zone and ended up having a miserable rainy day. We also chose glorious powder days on the ski slopes. We chose the difficulty of building an unconventional life from the ground up and the frustation of often feeling like we're circles in a square world. But we don't have a boss, we don't have to ask for time off and we can ski or travel to our heart's content.

This is the life that we chose. In a moment in time we chose it. Everyday, we continue to choose it. We continue to choose this life through every storm and every difficulty because the advantages far outweigh the drawbacks.

What's holding you back?

What would it take for you to begin living epicly?

What would it take for you to make one epic choice today?

When will you begin the process of reinventing your life?

It's never been easier.

The internet has made the world flat. If you want to make a living remotely, you can do it. Looking for people to encourage you, coach you, support you, challenge you? There's a cadre of bloggers you can turn to. There are Facebook groups where you can connect with people who share your goals and values. There's Skype and Google hangouts and an almost limitless number of resources for you to get whatever you need to begin living a life of your own design.

Today.

Thanks for reading. Now go do something. I do not wish you success. "Success" is just an impostor anyway.

I wish you a life of adventure.

Clark Vandeventer
Santa Barbara, April 28, 2015

Epicly or Epically?

What's the proper way to spell this variant of the word epic?

By now you've probably caught on that I'm not really big on being proper, so I spell it "epicly." I know this drives you pencil pushers out there crazy, so I figured I better address this so you don't think there's a typo every time you see the word appear in this book. It's spelled that way on purpose.

I've always preferred to spell it epicly, but my editor, Elizabeth Glass Turner, corrected it to epically throughout the book. I finally accepted her edits, but then hated the way it looked. This is my book and I figured I really shouldn't hate something about it.

I asked my friends on Facebook what they thought, and people were pretty much evenly divided. Some hated epicly and thought it was confusing. Some hated epically and thought it was confusing.

One person suggested epicklee. I've always liked epicly because I think it's more visually appealing, but one friend said she thought epically was more visually appealing. The only thing I learned was that asking this question on Facebook did not help me at all.

I did agree with one friend, though, who wrote that epicly is better because it is instantly recognizable. "Spelling is for communication, and if one way communicates better, use that way."

I was already inclined to believe my friend. He was singing my tune.

Therefore, epicly it is.

Sorry if it drives you crazy.

At least I didn't go with epicklee.

Who needs to read unWorking?

Meet twelve people who absolutely must read *unWorking*.

Recently laid off Roger

Roger is 40 years-old and was just laid off from his job. Roger made good money. Enough to have a decent place to live and a nice car to drive. Kids were in daycare and school. Roger and his wife could go out often enough but he could never get ahead. Now, he knows he should be out there trying to find another job, but he's worried. He's worried because he sees his industry changing and he's not sure how secure any job really is. And even if he could get a new job, does he really want to sign up for the grind again? Roger needs a new plan. Where can he find the help he needs to devise a new plan? In *unWorking*.

Daydreaming Danna

Danna just turned 30. She's got a great job and her peers hold her in high regard. She's good at what she does, but she often finds herself daydreaming about quitting her job to do something different. She's afraid. Where can she find the courage to pursue her dreams? She needs someone to explain to her how pursuing her dream is no less dangerous than the "safe" path she's currently on. Where can she find this help? In *unWorking*.

Moving back in with the folks Max

Max is in his late 20's and is suddenly out of work and moving back in with his parents. Maybe Max's parents buy him this book, but they should not if they want Max back out on his feet fast. If Max's parents want him out of the house ASAP, they encourage him to go get a job. But if Max's parents are happy to have him around, Max has an unbelievable opportunity. Max has time to figure things out without the pressure of having to come up with this month's rent. *unWorking* is his guide to lifestyle design.

Long-term unemployed Dan

A recent Wall Street Journal article titled, *Out of a Job, Some Decide to Take a Hike,* noted the growing segment of long-term unemployed who are deciding to do something different than sit on the couch and wait for the phone to ring. The article opens:

Unable to find steady work in a dismal Florida job market, Dan Kearns did something a lot of gainfully employed Americans can only dream of: Ditch the straight life and hike the length of the Appalachian Trail. Shouldering a 50-pound backpack, the 32-year-old construction worker hopped onto the trail in April at Neels Gap, Ga., joining other "through-hikers" bound for the AT's northern end point, nearly 2,200 miles away in Maine's Baxter State Park. He sold his car for $1,000 to finance the first leg of the trip, relying after that on handouts and the occasional farm job -- often backbreaking work weeding vegetable beds *or rolling bales of hay. "I wouldn't do this if I was employed," the New Jersey native explains. "I couldn't find any work, so I just decided to take a walk."*

unWorking is the perfect book for Dan to bring along with him on the trail. He's already exited the traditional path. He realizes the world has changed and that it's time to think differently. *unWorking* will give him the guidance he desperately needs to create a new life in the ~~emerging~~ already here world.

Mid-life crisis Melanie

Melanie has always been the light in any room that she enters. In high school she was popular, but not in the cliquish kind of way. She majored in English literature in college and went on a few shoestring tours of Europe during her summer vacations. She has a wonderful husband and great kids. She feels bad even thinking this because really her life is great... but she thought her life was going to be so much more. She thought her life was going to be *epic*. She wants it to be epic. Melanie should push through the crowds to get a copy of *unWorking*.

High School Grad Holly

Holly won't buy this book. Her parents won't buy it for her either because they want Holly to go to college and major in something practical like business or accounting. But Holly has an eccentric uncle who'd like to see Holly build her life around her passions instead of doing what everyone else does. When Uncle Davey comes to Holly's high school graduation open house, what does he bring as a gift? He brings *unWorking*.

High School Guidance Counselor Hal

Hal's never known what to do with those kids who don't fit the mold. Now he's got *unWorking*.

Homeschooled Harriet

Harriet is 17 years old and part of the fast growing home-school movement: home schoolers think differently than their traditionally schooled counterparts and are sometimes considering a life path that does not include college. How can they build a successful life without conforming to the traditional work mold? That's exactly what Harriet will find in *unWorking*.

College Grad Carlos

Carlos just graduated from college and he's entering the job market. Whatever choice he makes regarding his first job, he's sort of casting his lot. He's choosing a path. He's investing himself and his life. Based upon Carlos' decision, we can predict with some pretty good accuracy what his life will look like in ten years. Before Carlos chooses a path, he better make sure he knows what he wants life to look like, now and in ten years. Where can he find a guide to help him sort all this out? In *unWorking*.

Jeff Bezos

That's right, Jeff Bezos, CEO of Amazon.com absolutely needs to read this book! Since he's probably an Amazon Prime member, he'll even have it in two days with no extra shipping charges. Jeff Bezos, though, needs this book by the case. Each year, Amazon.com offers to pay their employees to quit. Once a year, they ask their employees, "Do you really want to work here?" If the answer is no, they'll pay the employee up to $5,000 to quit. Jeff Bezos says he does this "to encourage folks to take a moment and think about what they really want. In the long run, an employee staying somewhere they don't want to be isn't healthy for the employee or the company." A person who says, "You know, I'm not where I want to be..." and takes Bezos' offer is thinking about what they want in life. They're on the path to lifestyle design. How do they take the next step? They read *unWorking*. Jeff Bezos should give copies of the book for his staff who choose to stay with the company as well. CEOs of corporations should want their employees reading this book as a means to attract and keep people on their team who are passionate about their work.

Human Resources Specialist Hope

Hope's got a tough job. She has to figure out how to give someone who's just been laid off hope for their future. That's why Hope buys a case of *unWorking* and gives it to employees after they have been laid off.

Adventurous Addy

Addy just likes a good story.

Acknowledgements

"There is nothing to writing," according to Ernest Hemingway. "All you do is sit down at a typewriter and bleed." He also said that we should "write hard and clear about what hurts."

I wrote my first draft of this book on an iPad, and completed the second draft and succeeding drafts on a MacBook. Unlike Hemmingway, no typewriters were involved in the writing of this book. There were times however, I felt like I was opening a vein. To my parents, I want to say that I am sorry if portions of this book were painful for you to read. Those portions were painful for me to write. I continue to be indebted to you for so many things, not least of which being your encouragement of me as a writer from a young age.

Writing the acknowledgements to a book feels a bit like an Academy Awards speech, not that I've ever given an Academy Awards speech. It's just that I have so many people to thank.

First, what can I say about my wife? She's traveled this journey with me and together we have done some pretty special things. I can't imagine this life without her. On a practical level, she helped make this book possible by giving me the space to write. I first tried to write this book in the winter of 2011-12. I was going to take a morning a week to write, but I could never get into a groove. I am glad it did not work out at the time because I wasn't ready. There was still a lot of figuring out going on. The following winter, I was ready to write, but I felt like I needed to write and write and not stop until I was done. Monica took the kids to Santa Barbara for two weeks and in those two weeks I completed the first draft of this book. I skied all day and thought about what I was going to write while I was on the chairlift. Then, when I got home at night, I would write. The following winter (2013-14) Monica took the kids to Santa Barbara again and I completed the second draft of the book. Throughout the winter of 2014-15 and into the spring as we moved toward a final draft there were seemingly endless edits and again, Monica was a great support to me in this process. I'm very thankful to have a life partner to have created such an incredible life with and thankful to her for supporting me and encouraging me to write this book. Monica also helped me create the take-aways and the action items at the end of each chapter and helped manage the process of bringing the book to print.

I am also deeply indebted to Elizabeth Glass Turner. Elizabeth was not only my editor, she was my friend and counselor. She took my first draft and challenged me, told me what didn't make sense and helped me flesh out many sections that were raw and unfinished. She made me dig deeper and her own life experiences brought a lot of great perspective. She worked on each draft of this book with an editors' pen, but she was so much more than just an editor. I can look far and wide and it is hard for me to find a better friend than Elizabeth, who's been by my side, even if at a distance, since our college days at Indiana Wesleyan University. She didn't just dot the i's and cross the t's, she helped make this book what it is.

I owe a special thanks to Justin Mussler and Erik Fisher for pushing me to "get my book out there" -- to get it off my MacBook and into print. Every time I worked on the book, it got better. There comes a point, though, where you have to say, "This is it. These are my words. Here I stand." I also want to thank Jim Woods for setting me on course as we moved the book toward publication.

I am grateful to Greg Stielstra for helping me realize this book wasn't about me, but about lifestle design and how people could achieve an *unWorking* lifestyle. I'm also grateful to Tim Goeglein for his encouragement with the book and his affirmation that I'd created something special. I also want to think Kristen Miller Ferrall who was one of the final readers of this book before it was formatted for print. Her testimony about how the book spoke to her life helped sustain me as I dealt with the nagging practicalities and difficulties of publishing.

Besides my wife, the person I've talked with about the ideas presented in this book more than anyone is my friend Bryan Rosner. Bryan and I think very much alike in certain ways, but differently in others. Our conversations together have brought so much clarity to my thinking. I'm thankful for his friendship. What I appreciate most about Bryan is that he's open to new ideas and he wants to live deliberately. Bryan also owns a publishing company (in a completely unrelated field to this book) and his publishing advise was invaluable.

In 2011 when Monica and I started our blog FamilyTrek.org, we had no idea that our family travel blog would morph into a blog about family travel *and* lifestyle design. More than 500 blog posts later, we count our readers as trusted friends. No blog post is definitive. Much like the conversations I have over a cup of coffee with my friend Bryan, the blog posts on FamilyTrek.org are a conversation. They're all part of the process of sorting through life, living deliberately and achieving lifestyle design. We've had the opportunity to meet many readers as well as other bloggers in different corners of the world and it's always been a joy. Each individual has played a part in this book.

One or our FamilyTrek.org readers, Kelli Kennedy, also helped with edits of the book, and I am grateful to her for her help. She's a long-time reader, and it always brings a smile to my face whenever I see her name pop up on Facebook after she's liked or commented on a post on the Family Trek Facebook page.

And to Mr. Babbitt, who told me as a senior in high school that I had the soul of a writer, thank you.

Finally, here I am once again saying thanks to my in-laws. They've bought a lot of Clark stock over the years. I hope it pays off, but mainly, it feels good knowing someone believes in me.

From the Blog

WHY I'M A DAD NOW

This blog post can be found online at:

http://www.familytrek.org/why-im-a-dad-now/

I was exhausted, and I wasn't the one who had just given birth to a 10 pound, 6 ounce baby. It was the wee hours of the morning and after having a few hours with our first-born son the nurses took him to the nursery so we could get some sleep.

A few hours later a doctor came in and told us our son was being transferred to the NICU. I didn't even know what the NICU was and I was trying to hang onto the doctors' words and understand what he was telling us. We went back to sleep and the next morning

I would learn what those letters stood for. Neonatal Intensive Care Unit.

As we approached our son we had a lot of mixed emotions looking at him through the incubator with all those monitors on him. I watched his chest move up and down rapidly as he struggled to get the oxygen he needed. He had meconium aspiration, a condition caused when a newborn baby breathes in meconium and amniotic fluid into the lungs as the baby is being born. It's usually caused by stress during the delivery when the baby is not getting enough blood or oxygen. I guess those three hours my wife spent pushing were a little stressful for our son.

With all that meconium in his lungs there was not much room left for oxygen. The next few hours were spent learning what was going on and what we could expect and hope for moving forward. It was scary. Looking back it seems obvious to me that he was going to be just fine. Reflecting on that moment, I just remember being terrified.

A week later we brought him home.

My life has never been the same.

I'm a dad. There are many roles I play but I'm arranging my life to first and foremost be a husband to my wife and a dad to my kids. I suppose you could say I've given up potential income, career opportunities and social status.

And all I've gained are High 5's for going pee on the toilet from my son and sloppy kisses from my daughter.

Did you know that my sweet little girl adores me?

Being a dad makes mundane tasks like going to Wal-Mart a great adventure.

A few months after our first son was born I quit my job. I left a lucrative, enviable position to pursue a passion I held deep down within me. It didn't work out. I didn't have a Plan B so I quickly developed a new Plan A. It worked. Sort of. For a while.

And slowly the chase for a new career or business opportunity or more money began to take a back seat to lifestyle. Don't get me wrong. I'm an entrepreneur. I can't escape that. It's in my DNA. But you know all those stories you hear about guys at the end of their life reflecting about what they wish they'd done differently?

Wishing they'd spent more time with their family.

Wishing they'd gone on that camping trip with their family.

Been with his son when he took his first solo turns on skis.

Taught his daughter how to dance.

Read more bedtime stories.

That's not going to be me.

There are bills to be paid, sure. You have to pay the mortgage or the rent. You have to put food on the table and gas in the tank. The kids need shoes and clothes and diapers. And I need a drink when we put them to bed.

But I've chosen to not make the chase for the bigger house in a better neighborhood or a second car (my wife and I have shared a car for over 2 years), or a desire for any other material possession to rob me of the most valuable thing I can imagine: time with my kids.

People who don't live in my world or share my mindset have a hard time understanding me. On just about any afternoon you can find me doing something fun with my kids. My friends with 9-5 jobs think I'm on a perpetual vacation. But I get up early in the morning. I go to bed late at night. And I have an iPhone for all the times in-between.

It's not always easy. There are long days when my wife and I are juggling the kids and our shared and separate professional responsibilities and I think about how much easier life would be if I could just escape for 8-11 hours 5 days a week and collect a paycheck.

There are time periods, some painfully long, when money is tight.

A few years ago my wife and I rented out our home and traveled for six months with our son. We spent the first 3 weeks in Tahoe where my wife's family has a cabin. We were there to ski and nothing is more depressing in a ski town than rain in February. And it was raining. We were in the doldrums, little money in hand, and I turned to my wife and in a sort of depressed tone I said to her, "This is the life we chose."

Fast-forward just a few days. A cold front has brought in fresh powder and we are on the ski slopes. My wife and I get away for a morning while a friend watches our son and as we get ready to push-off to start down the slope on fresh powder I turn to my wife and I say, in a much different tone, "this is the life we chose."

It's not just the life we chose. It's the life we choose.

We chose this life at a moment in time. But at any moment we could abandon our choice. There are moments of weakness when I'm ready to cry "uncle." But each day our actions continue to be a reflection of our continual choosing.

I provide for my family. I don't have a lot of money in the bank. I once had a decent retirement account but I cashed that out in a failed entrepreneurial effort. All, well. I'll build it up again.

But do you know what happened after lunch today? My three-year-old (Jackson) picked up my briefcase and started walking toward the car.

Jackson: "I'm going to work!"

Me: "Oh, ok. You gonna make some money?"

Jackson: "No, no make money."

Me: "Yeah, that's the way it goes sometimes."

It's a stupid moment in time. A silly moment with my three-year-old.

And he'll only be three once.

That's why I'm a dad now.

ABOUT THAT WHOLE PROTESTANT WORK ETHIC THING...

This blog post can be found online at:

http://www.familytrek.org/about-that-whole-protestant-work-ethic-thing/

I was listening to a politician speak recently when he started talking about the value of the good old American work ethic. He said his dad never had to teach him about work ethic, that he had learned it by watching him. His dad was up every morning before sunrise. He left the house before all the kids were up. He worked long hours and didn't come home till the sun went down.

I thought to myself, "the guy never saw his dad."

I don't want to trivialize how hard life can be and the need at times to adjust to the cards life deals us. I remember a season of my childhood when my dad was working three jobs to try to hold onto the life he'd built up for us. The whole idea of the Protestant work ethic, which America was supposedly built on, has been on my mind recently, though. The tagline of our blog is "Our quest to **work less**, live more, and travel the world as a family."

What's my problem with work?

It's not that I have a problem with work. In fact, I rather enjoy working. I get satisfaction out of my work and it brings real meaning to my leisure. *I'm just not sure what we call an "ethic" — the Protestant or American work ethic — is an ethic at all.*

I can hear the chorus now. **"How can providing for your family not be an ethic? How can you not place value on that? How can you not champion *that*?"**

First, let's clarify what providing for one's family means. Are we talking about basic needs? Food. Shelter. Clothing. Medical care. I champion parents who do whatever it takes to provide these things for their kids. Trust me, I'm a dad… I get the desire to give everything to your kids. But it doesn't take long for "providing for my kids" to slide into second cars and second mortgages. Soon, the late model Ford just isn't good enough and it's time for a new car. Soon, the neighborhood you're living in isn't nice enough and the house isn't big enough either.

Is that stuff really for the kids? My wife and I have adopted a patchwork income approach to providing for our family's needs. Because of our lifestyle choice, we get to spend a lot of time together as a couple and a lot of time together as a family. There are times, however, when we just have to work. I have to go out and see clients or one of us just needs to take the computer and go to Starbucks for a few hours to work. Our kids get that. And here's a common dialogue in our house:

Me: Hey, Jackson, mommy has to go to work. We're just going to hang out for a while. Just you, Emery, and me."

Jackson: Why does mommy have to go to work?

Monica: I'm going to go to work so we can make some money to have things that we need and to do fun things.

Jackson: No, I want you to stay here.

Jackson is 4 and he may not get the fact that his mom and I have to work in order to live in the house that we do. The bunk-beds that he and his sister love cost money. All the travels we do together as a family that he loves take money. All those hot dogs he'll eat at the beach this summer cost money. But when given a basic choice between time with his mom and dad or our family having more money…. he chooses time with us every day of the week and twice on Sunday.

The sad thing is that I know people who are hiding behind either that good ol' fashioned American work ethic or the life they say they're providing for their kids… and all their kids want is them, *not the money and the stuff that they're trading themselves for.*

We need to knock work down a notch. It's not a glorious thing. It's not a cross to bear. It's just a means to an end.

We talk about people who have a strong work ethic with such admiration, "Michael is such a hard worker. His family is lucky to have such a hard working dad…." When I hear things like this I often think to myself, "Poor Michael either hasn't figured out how the world works or he's avoiding his family by putting in long hours. Neither of these are admirable. It's just sad."

We applaud the wrong behavior, the intent not the result, and our society has pushed people to work so hard that they can't wait until they can someday retire, if they don't end up working themselves to death.

Rather than putting my nose to the grindstone and missing these years with my family, I'd rather live a life now I never want to retire from. My work brings meaning to my life. My family brings meaning to my life. My traveling brings meaning to my life. My faith and friendships bring meaning to my life. Why would I want to retire from this? I choose to live this life now rather than waiting till tomorrow because tomorrow isn't guaranteed to me and even if it comes my kids will be grown.

What do you think? Is the American, Protestant Work ethic an *ethic* at all?

WHY I TOOK MY DAUGHTER ON A TRIP SHE'LL NEVER REMEMBER

This blog post can be found online at:

http://www.familytrek.org/why-i-took-my-daughter-on-a-trip-shell-never-remember/

Hardly anyone has ever heard of the sleepy little beach town of Khanom, Thailand. From the beach you can see the island of Koh Samui, a hugely popular tourist destination that attracts more than two million visitors each year. For a month, we were making our home in Khanom. Our little family with three kids ranging in age from 6 to 1 spent our days swimming in the ocean and cruising around town on our motorbike.

At a local hangout we met Toon and arranged for him to take us to Khao Sok National Park. This was a big excursion, which included a lot of time in Toon's car, but we would see some of the stuff we'd come to the other side of the world to see. We'd ride elephants, canoe down rivers, and sleep in the floating houses on the dam.

Now, back home in America, I look back at those two days as two of the best of our time in Thailand. Heck, those were two of the best days of my life.

After we emerged from our few days in the jungle I posted a photo on Facebook of me with my 1-year-old daughter Abigail with the following caption:

I know she'll never remember this trip. That's not the point. I want our travels to shape the woman she becomes.

It got a lot of "likes" but I feel like I need to elaborate.

We've loaded our kids on planes, trains, and automobiles to far corners of the world for a reason. I know my daughter Abigail will never remember this recent trip to Thailand or any of the other trips we take in the next few years. That's not the point. I want our travels to shape the woman she becomes. I want her to see, before she is able to develop an idea of what's "normal," that America isn't the world. I want her to see people living differently than we do in America and speaking different languages and eating different foods. That's no judgement of America. I just want my kids to understand the world is bigger, and if I have the power to expose them to these things (and I do), I want them to see this while their view of the world is still very much being formed.

There is another reason, though, that we travel with our young kids.

My daughter will never remember this trip, but I will.

I will remember carrying Abigail through one of the oldest rainforest in the world. I will remember trying to console her as our long-tail boat zipped across the dam. I'll remember her delight when she saw the pink dolphin rise to surface of the ocean. I'll remember how the first time she ever swung on a big kid swing by herself was at a park in Bangkok. I'll remember the way she treated beggars on the street and our hotel desk staff exactly the same. I'll remember trying to hold her tightly and keep her asleep while we transferred from a ferry to a car. I'll remember her riding on me in the baby carrier while I cruised across town on my motorbike.

There were times while we were in Thailand -- several times actually -- when we would think about doing something and we'd say, "That'd be great if it were just us and the kids, but it would be a nightmare with Abby..." Sometimes we decided to do it anyway, sometimes we skipped the outing altogether, and sometimes just

Monica or me would do something with the kids while one of us stayed with Abby.

I'm happy for all those times, though. It's important for the kids to see that Abby is a part of our family and that we need to consider her needs as we plan our activities and there's no activity I missed in Thailand that compares to being my kids' dad.

One night I was walking back to our place on the island of Koh Tao and saw this romantic little restaurant. I thought about how much I'd enjoy going to dinner there with my wife. That just wasn't in the cards, though. Not on this trip; not with the kids in tow. But then I thought about how un-unique that romantic little restaurant really was. I've been to so many romantic little restaurants with my wife. What we did earlier that day -- snorkeling and watching the kids point out different species of fish in utter amazement -- that was unique! That was special.

We've been traveling with our kids longer than any of them can remember. Our son Jackson, now six years old, is on his second passport. When we're talking with friends they'll often say things to us like, "I can't imagine traveling the way you do with young kids." This is all our kids have ever known, though. This is just what they do.

Jackson and Emery have figured out how to navigate a metro system and how to hail a taxi. They're figuring out the world. Abby is too. So am I.

I am happy to do it with them. What a great adventure.

Read more of Clark's writings on lifestyle design,
as well as stories of his
family's travels around the world
at FamilyTrek.org and like Family Trek
on Facebook at facebook.com/FamilyTrek.

About the Author

By the time he was 26-years-old, Clark Vandeventer was the deputy director of the Reagan Ranch and had raised millions of dollars to preserve the home of the 40th President of the United States, Ronald Reagan.

Just as the early birth pangs of The Great Recession were being felt, Clark realized he was no longer passionate about his work. With reckless abandon, he quit his job. Trudging through the Great Recession, by 2010, Clark was a candidate for United States Congress.

He bet big on winning, putting all other work on hold and cashing out his retirement to be a full time candidate. When he lost his election, he was out of money and out of work. Two months after being a rising political star and candidate for Congress, Clark moved his wife and two young children into his in-laws garage.

That's when Clark began the process of reinventing his life.

Today, Clark and his wife Monica, enjoy a lifestyle of design through patchwork income, spending winters in Lake Tahoe where they ski, and the rest of the year free to move about the world wherever their hearts desire.

When he's not blogging, skiing, or traveling with his family, Clark is a consultant to non-profit organizations, training professional staff how to raise big bucks for their causes. You can learn more at MajorGiftsFundraiser.com. Follow him on twitter @clarkvand.

Keep the conversation going...

You can read more of Clark's writings on lifestyle design, as well as stories of his family's travels around the world at FamilyTrek.org. You can also like Family Trek on Facebook at facebook.com/FamilyTrek. If you find yourself in Tahoe, check out TahoeSkiBum.com, which is published by Clark and his wife Monica.

You can also go to unWorkingBook.com to purchase additional copies of this book at a discount. We'd also love to hear your thoughts on the book and how it has impacted your life. Share your thoughts on Twitter with the hashtag #unWorkingBook or tag Clark @clarkvand.

You can invite Clark to speak or arrange for a book-signing in your area. For more information, go to unWorkingBook.com.

Did you love this book? Leave a review on Amazon.com and Clark will send you a virtual high-five.

Go to unWorkingBook.com and sign up to receive emails from Clark.